QUICK & EASY PROJECTS
FOR THE WEEKEND CARPENTER

QUICK & EASY PROJECTS
FOR THE WEEKEND
CARPENTER

*Over 25 simple & stylish pieces
to make for your home*

ALAN & GILL BRIDGEWATER

NEW
HOLLAND

This edition first published in 2003 by New Holland
Publishers (UK) Ltd
London • Cape Town • Sydney • Auckland

www.newhollandpublishers.com

86-88 Edgware Road, London W2 2EA, United Kingdom

80 McKenzie Street, Cape Town, 8001, South Africa

14 Aquatic Drive, Frenchs Forest, NSW 2086, Australia

218 Lake Road, Northcote, Auckland, New Zealand

ISBN 1 85974 446 X

Editorial direction: Rosemary Wilkinson
Project editor: Kate Latham
Production: Caroline Hansell

Designed and created for New Holland by AG&G Books
Illustrator: Gill Bridgewater
Project design: Alan and Gill Bridgewater
Photography: Ian Parsons
Editor: Fiona Corbridge
Woodwork: Alan and Glyn Bridgewater

AG&G Books would like to thank *Axminster™ Power Tool
Centre* for supplying the pictures on pages 8 and 9.

Reproduction by PICA Colour Separation, Singapore
Printed and bound in Singapore by Tien Wah Press (Pte)
Ltd

The information in this book is true and complete to
the best of our knowledge. All recommendations are
made without guarantee on the part of the authors
and the publishers. The authors and publishers disclaim
any liability for damages or injury resulting from the
use of this information.

Contents

Introduction

Sometimes, when I am busy in my workshop, with the warm, nutty smell of wood filling the air, I think about all the pleasures of woodwork. Of course the hands-on procedures are fun to do, but on top of that, I am always amazed by the fact that I may have a whole heap of wood stacked in the corner on one day, and by the next it has been transformed into a beautiful piece of furniture. When I watch the various projects being used in the house, or when I give them to friends and family as gifts, it is very rewarding to know that, but for me, the items wouldn't exist.

The intention of this book is to share with you all the pleasures of building projects from wood. When I first sat down to think up the projects, I was overwhelmed with ideas – there were so many exciting possibilities. Aimed specifically at keen weekend carpenters, the projects are carefully directed, with plenty of options, thorough step-by-step directions, and most important of all, they can be made and finished in the space of a weekend. We have designed the projects so that they can be made by woodworkers at all levels, from inexperienced beginners with a basic tool kit, to more accomplished woodworkers who want to make something that little bit special. We show you, in hands-on-tool detail, how to make over 25 different projects, including a bright, painted stool for a child, a chair for the porch or conservatory, a table, a chest, a rustic French cupbourd for the kitchen, and bread and cheese boards. Each project opens with an introduction to put the piece in context, and then we go straight into the making stages. There is a full-page photograph to show the piece in detail, step-by-step text and photographs, extensive tool, material and cutting lists, working drawings, design variations and tip boxes. We have done our best to see that you have a wonderful woodworking time every weekend, from ordering wood to setting out the designs and working with the router.

So now it is time to roll up your sleeves and get down to the fantastic, finger-tingling adventure of weekend carpentry. Best of luck.

Alan & Gill

Tools and equipment

Woodworking is an incredibly rewarding activity, but only if you are using the right tools and equipment for the task. It's no good battling on with the wrong-size bandsaw, or trying to smooth wood with a plane that is dull-edged, and then deciding that woodworking is not for you. If you choose your tools with care, you will enjoy the experience of woodworking. Buy a basic tool kit to begin with and purchase additional tools when the need arises.

BASIC MACHINES

Traditionally, home woodworkers used hand tools – planes, saws, hand drills and so on – but there is now a shift to using small, basic machines to do some of the more tedious tasks. The following five machines are very useful: circular saw, planer-thicknesser, bandsaw, bench drill press and scroll saw.

Circular saw A circular saw is a machine for sawing stock to width and length. It is a table with a saw disc at the centre, a rip fence to the right-hand side and a sliding table to the left. To use it, you true up one edge of the wood, set the rip fence to the desired width, and then use your hands and a push-stick to move the wood through. It's a good machine if you want to reduce costs by converting rough-sawn boards to various plank and batten widths.

Planer-thicknesser A planer-thicknesser is a combination machine that is designed to plane all sides and edges of the wood square to each other, working through each in turn. Professional woodworkers generally use two machines – a surface planer and a thicknesser – but home woodworkers usually opt for a dual-purpose planer-thicknesser. There are many machines on the market, so spend time looking at the options.

1 **Circular saw:** *A circular saw is a useful machine, especially if you are going to do a lot of woodwork. It is mainly used for converting large boards into smaller sections, with the benefit of speed and accuracy.*

2 **Portable thicknesser:** *A thicknesser is used for reducing sections to the desired thickness (or width).*
3 **Surface planer:** *A surface planer establishes flat planed surfaces on a face and an adjacent edge.*

Bandsaw An electric bandsaw is a benchtop machine made up of a flexible, looped blade running over and being driven by two or more wheels. It is designed for cutting broad curves in thick-section wood. (Narrow blades suit tight curves in thin wood, while wide blades are better for broad curves in thick wood.) I use a small bandsaw fitted with a 10 mm blade.

Bench drill press The bench drill press – sometimes also called a pillar drill – is a machine dedicated to drilling holes. While you might think that a small, hand-held electric drill is sufficient for this purpose, a good-size bench drill press is better, because it enables you to bore accurately placed holes every time. To use it, you fit the bit in the chuck, clamp the workpiece to the drill table, set the depth gauge, and then pull the capstan wheel to bore the hole. A bench drill press teamed with a forstner bit is a combination that is difficult to beat.

Scroll saw The scroll saw is a fine-bladed electric saw designed for cutting intricate curves in wood. Before using it, the blade is tensioned, and then the workpiece is fed towards the blade. In order to saw out a shape in the middle of a piece of wood, one end of the blade is detached and passed through a drilled hole.

SPECIAL MACHINES

There are of course many other types of woodworking machine – everything from joint cutters, sanders and veneering presses through to spindle moulders, tenon cutters, large and small lathes, and plenty more besides. Novice woodworkers usually find that they soon develop an interest and expertise in a particular area, so they then go on to buy appropriate small machines. For example, I very quickly became interested in woodturning – so much so that I purchased a lathe, and then a large, slow-wheel grinder to sharpen my turning tools. If you get hooked on joint making, for example, you might choose to buy a dedicated mortiser and a machine for cutting dovetails, and then a special machine to hone your chisels, and so on. My advice is that you should not rush out straight away and start buying large lumps of machinery, because they might never get used. Also, don't be tempted to purchase small add-on attachments for your basic power tools (see page 10), because they can never perform as well as a dedicated machine. It is much better to borrow machines from your friends if they are necessary to follow these projects, and then to buy your own equipment when you fully appreciate your needs.

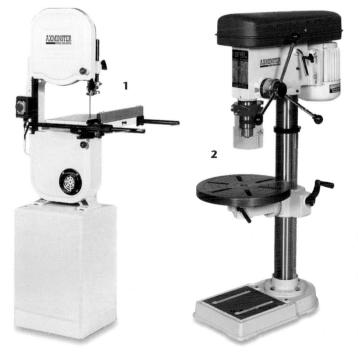

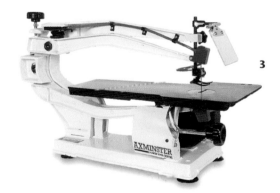

1 **Bandsaw:** *A bandsaw is ideal for reducing rough-sawn planks and cutting broad curves in thick wood.*
2 **Bench drill press:** *A bench drill press, used in conjunction with a forstner bit, enables you to make accurate, clean-sided holes.*
3 **Scroll saw:** *A scroll saw is the best machine for cutting tight curves and intricate fretwork designs.*

BASIC POWER TOOLS

Many novice woodworkers own an electric drill and various attachments such as a sanding disc, mini lathe, dovetail cutter and drill stand, all of which work in conjunction with the drill. The problem with these add-ons is that although they do work, to a greater or lesser extent, the results are usually so disappointing that the woodworker soon becomes disenchanted. My advice is to buy dedicated power tools, designed specifically to do a task, when you are confident that you can make good use of them. In the context of this book, the following six power tools are the ones to consider: cordless drill, jigsaw and sander (basic tools), router, mitre circular saw and biscuit jointer (special tools).

Cordless drill A cordless drill is a great tool, which is perfect for jobs where you don't want to be hampered by a trailing power cable. I have two such drills – one small and the other large. My large drill has a torque facility that allows me to use it both for drilling holes and for driving in screws. All I do is turn the numbered setting to suit the load and the depth of the screw, and then get on with the job. The battery size allows me to work for most of the day without recharging it. However Gill finds the weight of this drill a bit heavy on the wrists, and prefers to use the much smaller drill, which has the battery unit built into the handle. At the end of the day, you have to remember to plug the rechargeable battery into the mains.

However, bear in mind that while a cordless drill does free the working area from power cables, the gearing of the drill requires that you work the holes in gentle stages, rather than single thrusts.

Jigsaw A jigsaw looks a little bit like a sander with a flat table on the underside, from which a blade protrudes. To use it, the saw table is set on the workpiece, with the blade not quite touching the wood to be cut, then the power is switched on and the tool is advanced. As the blade jiggles up and down, it swings from front to back so that it is clear of the wood on the down stroke. On most saws the table can be adjusted so that it tilts and allows you to cut at an angle of up to 45°. Some jigsaws

are able to cut a thickness of up to 100 mm, so it is a very useful tool for most of the projects in this book.

Sander Modern sanders are really very sophisticated. You have a choice between wheel sanders, belt sanders, sanders with file-like fingers, random orbital sanders that fit in the palm of your hand, large high-powered sanders that are used for finishing wide areas, and so on. We have two machines: a large, flat sander that we use for working broad surfaces, and a little triangular palm-size sander that is good for rounding over edges and for getting into tight corners.

SPECIAL POWER TOOLS

Router A router is designed to do all the tasks that were once achieved by using a whole range of planes. Not so long ago, grooves, moulding, rebates and tongues were cut with chisels and different-sized planes (with various universal and multi-planes coping with a number of tasks). Nowadays, a router does all these things. There are two schools of thought about routers. One says that they are noisy, dusty, potentially very dangerous, altogether unpleasant, and the cutters are very expensive; the other says that they are wonderful. Using a router may not be as much fun as using a plane, and the results may not be any better, but there is no denying that they are very much faster.

To perform the tasks, a router is fitted with cutters in various shapes and sizes, which are the reverse of the shape that you want to cut. So, for example, a tongue-shaped cutter will make a groove-shaped cut. A router can be used as a hand-held tool and run forward to make the cut, or it can be turned over and fitted in a router table, in which case the workpiece is moved so that it comes into contact with the cutter.

Mitre circular saw Strictly speaking, a power tool is defined as a smallish, hand-held tool such as a router, drill or sander, but some of the benchtop machines are now so small and portable that the distinction between them is becoming blurred. The mitre circular saw looks a bit like a cross between an angle grinder and a guillotine. It is primarily designed to crosscut, but you can also cut mitres and angles through to 45°. The length of timber is set on the table, the power is switched on and the blade is lowered or pulled across the wood.

Biscuit jointer The biscuit jointer, or biscuiter, is a versatile, easy-to-use tool. You simply make marks on the two pieces of wood that you want to join (edge to edge or at right angles), then set the jointer on the mark, press the button and push forward. This causes a saw wheel to make a groove. Next, you align grooves in both pieces of wood, fill them with glue, slide in a little biscuit-shaped piece of compressed wood, and clamp the wood together. This forms a reinforced joint.

Useful power tools: *1 Jigsaw for cutting curves, 2 Router for cutting grooves, joints and edge profiles (cutters: 3 Radius cutter for routing an edge profile, 4 Straight cutter for trimming edges, 5 Straight cutter for routing grooves and housings, 6 Chamfer cutter for routing a 45° bevel), 7 Palm sander for smoothing flat or shaped surfaces (with 8 Sanding sheet), 9 Rechargeable drill and screwdriver.*

WORKING SAFELY

Woodworking is potentially dangerous so always follow this safety checklist:
- Do not use machinery if you are too tired to concentrate or taking medication that makes you drowsy.
- Study the machine manuals.
- Keep electric cables and plugs on power tools in good condition.
- Let someone in the house know when you are using any machines.
- Make sure you are adequately protected with a dust mask, goggles and ear defenders (see page 13).
- If you have long hair, tie it back.
- Supervise children.
- Keep a first-aid kit nearby.
  - Be near a telephone in case of accidents.
  - Keep the workshop locked.

HAND TOOLS

Weekend carpenters need a good range of hand tools, including marking-out tools, saws, planes, chisels, hammers, mallets, knives and clamps.

Marking-out tools Woodwork starts with measurements and guidelines. You will need a tape measure, pencils and rule, a square, set square and bevel gauge for establishing angles, a pair of dividers for stepping off measurements, a pair of compasses for drawing circles, and a mortise gauge for setting out joints.

Saws The most useful saws to purchase are a tenon saw for sawing small sections of wood to length

and for cutting large details, a gents saw for small joints, and a mitre frame saw for cutting angles. Always choose best-quality saws that can be re-sharpened.

Planes You need three planes: a good smoothing plane for levelling board widths, planing edges and for skimming the ripples that can occur on machine-planed wood, a block plane for cleaning up end grain and for planing through tenons flush with a surface, and a spokeshave for planing curves.

Chisels A set of good-quality chisels is essential. While there are all manner of chisels on the market, I recommend that you get yourself a set of bevel-edge chisels – the best that you can afford. It is also useful to have a sharpening stone.

Frequently used hand tools and drill bits:

1 Mallet, 2 Mitre frame saw, 3 Swift-release clamp, 4 Sash clamp, 5 Metal rule or straightedge, 6 Smoothing plane, 7 Pin hammer, 8 Bevel gauge, 9 Mortise gauge, 10 Square, 11 File, 12 Turning tool, 13 Spokeshave, 14 Block plane, 15 Tape measure, 16 Dividers, 17 Pair of compasses, 18 Pencil, 19 Large penknife, 20 Small penknife, 21 Forstner drill bit, 22 Cross-point screwdriver, 23 Twist bit, 24 Plug cutter, 25 Pilot-countersink bit, 26 Allen key wrench, 27 Long-nosed pliers, 28 Adjustable wrench, 29 Electric soldering iron, 30 Bevel-edge chisel, 31 Gents saw, 32 Tenon saw, 33 Small hacksaw.

Hammers and mallets I use three different hammers: a large claw hammer for hefty work and for pulling out nails, and a couple of different-sized pin hammers for all the small nailing tasks. A mallet is suitable for the times when you need to strike the wood or a tool and be certain that it will not damage them or leave a mark. A carpenter's square-headed mallet is ideal for tapping chisels; a heavy, round-headed mallet provides more weight, or is good when using carving gouges.

Knives Knives are extremely useful tools. A good selection might include a small penknife for whittling, an old chip-carving knife for marking out and for tidying up tasks, and a large, bevel-bladed knife for cutting dowels. I find that an old knife tends to keep its edge longer. These can often be found in junk shops.

Clamps You can never have too many clamps. I use several long-beam sash clamps, a holdfast clamp on the workbench alongside the vice, one or two new swift-release clamps, and a whole host of G-clamps that I have collected over the years. Only buy the best, always get them in pairs, and don't be tempted to purchase them secondhand, or to buy cheap imports.

Metalworking tools As well as the woodworking tools, you will also need a small hacksaw for trimming nails and cutting threaded metal rod to length, a file for smoothing the sawn edges of these, and pliers for any number of tasks. (I also use an electric soldering iron for pyrography: it is not really designed for the task, but it is safe and it does the job efficiently.)

OTHER TOOLS

Drill bits You need twist bits for drilling general holes, and large-size forstner bits to make special holes that form part of the design. If you can afford it, get yourself a whole range of forstner bits. They are expensive, but last well and cut a perfect hole every time. You will also need a pilot-countersink bit for drilling screwholes for countersunk screws, and a counter-bore bit and matching plug cutter for making a screw joint that incorporates a recess for a wooden plug.

Woodturning tools If you want to try your hand at woodturning, you will first need a lathe, plus a selection of woodturning tools including gouges for rouging out, a skew chisel for cutting grooves and for smoothing up, a parting tool for parting off, and a couple of scrapers for general smoothing and tidying up. Start by making do with the tools supplied with the lathe, and then get yourself a better range when you have more experience and can decide what you really need.

SAFETY EQUIPMENT

When working with machines that make a lot of noise and produce fine dust, you need, at the very least, to get yourself a basic dust mask, a pair of ear defenders and a pair of safety goggles. I have also invested in a full-face respirator for working with the lathe. This mask not only allows me to wear my glasses, but it filters the air without the need to have something pressing directly against my mouth. There is one further health consideration: sometimes exotic species of wood cause allergic reactions. I avoid this possibility by mostly limiting myself to using pine (American or European pine).

Safety equipment: *1 Full-face respirator with built-in visor, dust filter and air blower, 2 Ear defenders, 3 Dust mask for low levels of wood dust, 4 Goggles.*

Materials

It is best to purchase wood from a specialist supplier – a company that only sells wood and related products and tools. It is no good expecting the local general DIY store to supply everything you require or to have a detailed knowledge of the products on sale. For the projects in this book, I advise you to purchase your wood ready prepared, and as near as possible to the finished size. Inspect the wood on offer closely and reject pieces that are split, of poor colour, twisted, full of knots or in any way faulted. If a piece of wood looks uncharacteristic, keep on searching. Go armed with a cutting list and a tape measure, and be clear in your own mind as to your needs. The ideal supplier is the sort of establishment staffed by friendly, knowledgeable people, who are prepared to cut the wood to size without splintering the cut edges, and can ensure that all the edges are square to each other. Certainly you will pay extra, but you won't be paying for wood that can't be used. Always ask for the offcuts.

WOOD TYPES

Swedish pine A straight-grained, creamy coloured softwood. It is easy to work, with an attractive grain texture and a minimum of knots – a perfect choice for most of the projects in this book.

Swedish laminated pine Whenever I have trouble getting a board wide enough, I generally use Swedish laminated pine. The pine is sawn into strips and glued to a prepared board width. It's a good product for component parts such as the sides of chests. Avoid using laminated pine for outdoor furniture.

Ash A long-grained, tough, grey to red-brown hardwood traditionally used when there is a need for strength. A good choice for many of the projects.

Maple A creamy-coloured hardwood – perfect for modern furniture. I used it for the Kitchen Trolley. It cuts to a beautiful crisp finish.

American oak Sometimes known as American red oak, this hardwood is pink-brown in colour, with a beautiful straight grain. Although it is a very tough wood, it's also relatively easy to work.

American cherry A creamy pink-to-brown, fine-textured, straight-grained hardwood. It is expensive, but a good choice if you require a hard, shiny finish. Specify American cherry, because it comes in much wider boards than the European species.

American mahogany A red-brown, straight-grained, uniform-textured hardwood. I avoid using mahogany, because it is an endangered species and I don't like all the fine dust, but I sometimes use offcuts salvaged from old doors. It's a good choice for very small details.

READY PREPARED WOOD

Ready prepared wood is planed and squared on all faces to a set width. You can also order it sized, and it will be sawn to a set length. However, if you enjoy the prospect of sawing and planing, just order the wood seasoned and sawn. When it comes to using tongue-and-groove boards (as in the French Cupboard), I go for best-quality prepared double-sided pine boards.

PLYWOOD

The projects in this book use top-quality birch plywood, which is a sheet material made up from veneer layers. It is easy to work – it saws and planes to a clean edge, and the light-coloured grain is very attractive.

SAMPLES OF WOOD TYPES AND FINISHES

Wood types (and finishes): *1 Swedish pine (teak oiled), 2 Ash (teak oiled), 3 Maple (teak oiled), 4 American oak (Danish oiled), 5 American cherry (Danish oiled), 6 American mahogany (Danish oiled), 7 American oak (wire-brushed and oiled), 8 Swedish pine (colourwashed), 9 Swedish pine (acrylic paint).*

FIXINGS

There are literally thousands of products on the market, but I generally limit myself to using steel and brass screws, nails and pins, plated steel threaded rod that I cut to length and use with washers and nuts, hex-head and toggle fasteners, wooden dowels, and plastic screw blocks. The brass hex-heads used in conjunction with the toggles and threaded rod may be unfamiliar to you. If you look at the Adjustable Porch Chair on pages 130–135, you will see how these beautiful fixings allow boards to be joined at right angles to each other, without the need to cut traditional joints, and with the added benefit that the structure can be disassembled for easy transport. Note that most modern fixings for making joints are designed to be hidden from view.

FITTINGS

The projects use four primary fittings: two different-shaped hinges (surface-mounted and recessed), brass cuphooks, and swivel wheels. There is not much to say about these items, other than they are best purchased when the project has been made, so that you can order a specific size and shape to fit the finished sizes. When you are buying hinges, obtain screws to fit at the same time. When it comes to knobs and handles, I much prefer to whittle my own from scraps of wood – as used on the Bathroom Cabinet (pages 88–93) and the French Cupboard (pages 124–129). I select a promising piece of wood, either a piece of straight-grained pine or a piece of lime, and then simply whittle away with a penknife until I have a shape that I like.

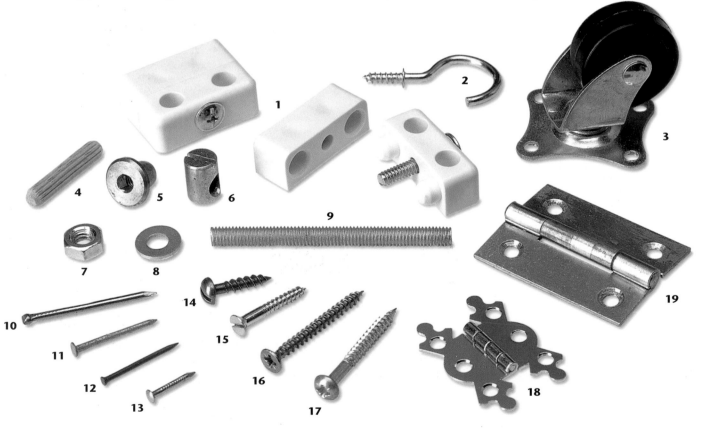

Useful fixings and fittings: *1 Plastic joining blocks, 2 Brass cuphook, 3 Swivel wheel, 4 Wooden fluted dowel, 5 Brass hex-head nut, 6 Toggle fastener, 7 Nut, 8 Washer, 9 Threaded rod (available in 1 m lengths), 10 Oval-headed nail, 11 Galvanized flat-headed nail,*

12 Black steel pin, 13 Brass round-headed pin, 14 Slotted round-headed screw, 15 Slot-headed countersunk screw, 16 Cross-headed countersunk screw, 17 Cross-headed, round-topped screw, 18 Surface-mounted hinge, 19 Recessed hinge with countersunk screwholes.

GLUE

There are hundreds of types of glue on the market, but there is no technical reason why, for the projects in this book, you shouldn't use white PVA glue. Squeeze it straight from the plastic bottle and smear it over both mating surfaces, and then clamp up and leave to cure.

FINISHING

Fortunately, thick, brown, high-shine varnishes are no longer in fashion. Instead we can use traditional finishes such as teak oil and Danish oil, or colourwashes in conjunction with oil and beeswax. The trouble with varnish is that you have to be careful there aren't any dribbles, and make sure that dust doesn't settle during the drying process. With oil, you don't have to worry about these things. I use teak oil and Danish oil straight from the bottle, either wiped on with a cloth or applied with a brush. Catalyst (two-part) lacquers are excellent spray finishes but unsuitable for the home workshop as special ventilation is required. Colourwash is made from acrylic paint thinned down with water. If I want to achieve a sheen finish, I simply wait for the oil or paint to dry, rub down with graded sandpapers, and then burnish with pure beeswax polish.

Glue and finishing materials: *1 PVA glue, 2 Teak oil, 3 Acrylic colourwash, 4 Danish oil, 5 Buffing polishing cloth, 6 Lint-free cotton cloth, 7 Pure beeswax polish, 8 Sanding block, 9 Garnet paper, 10 Silicon-carbide paper, 11 Aluminum oxide paper, 12 Wire brush.*

Basic techniques

Woodwork is a bit like a journey. It is wonderful to set out, and just as exciting to reach your destination, but a good part of the enjoyment is in all the adventures between start and finish. It is a great feeling when you present family or friends with something that you have made with your own two hands, but many of the procedures and techniques along the way are just as pleasurable. When I test the keenness of a razor-sharp edge, smell the wood and feel its texture, and then go on to make a crisp, clean cut, it is very satisfying. The following section will show you how to use your tools to achieve the various forms, joints and textures. If you are ever unsure about any procedures involving tools, or uncertain whether a type of wood is suitable, it is always a good idea to have a trial run on offcuts of wood. Try and keep the workshop shipshape – some woodworkers start a fresh project by cleaning and sharpening hand tools, tidying up the workshop and cleaning woodworking machines.

PREPARING PIECES OF WOOD

When you have decided what you want to make, take your carefully selected pieces of planed wood and sort them into groups. Mark each piece so that you know how it fits into the scheme of things, noting the top, bottom, best faces and edges. Use a pencil and rule to measure the lengths. Take a set square and run the marked points around the wood, so that you know which parts need to be cut away. Use a pair of compasses to set out curves and dividers to transfer measurements from drawings to the wood.

If you need to reduce the width of a board or set out a joint, adjust the marking gauge to the appropriate measurement and run the gauge along the wood to make a mark. Use the bevel gauge to set out lines that are going to run at an angle to an edge.

If you have pairs of components, mark them out at the same time so that they are identical (and remember to make them a mirror image of each other). When you are setting out a detailed joint, it helps if you score the lines with a knife. When you have set out all the lines that go to make up the design, it is often a good idea to shade in the waste side of the cutting line, so that you know precisely where to run the saw cut.

CUTTING CURVED SHAPES

To cut a curve, you have a choice of using a jigsaw, a scroll saw, a bandsaw or one of the hand saws. A jigsaw is best for cutting rough curves in thick wood, when the line of cut is well away from the edge of the workpiece (see Fig 1). Set the table part of the saw on the mark, switch on the power and advance to make the cut. Jigsaws have a tilting base, which changes the angle of the saw cut, and numerous types of blade are available to suit the type and thickness of a material.

FIG 1

Use a scroll saw for cutting fine curves in wood less than 50 mm thick (see Fig 2). Fit a new blade and adjust the tension until the blade "pings" when plucked. Set the workpiece on the saw table, switch on the power, and run the workpiece into the blade. If you feel the wood running off course, or you see the blade bending, ease back and readjust the direction of approach. If you need to cut out a window shape, then you can do one of two things. Either run the cut in from an edge or, to avoid cutting the wood surrounding the window, drill a hole through the waste, and then unhitch the saw blade, pass it through the hole and re-tension as already described.

out several times to remove the waste and to minimize overheating. If you are faced with drilling lots of holes in lots of identical component parts (see the Sauna Bench project on pages 98–101), it's a good idea to build a jig from offcuts (a "fence" and a "stop" screwed to a base board, which is clamped to the drill table).

An electric drill used with a twist bit is a good option when you want to drill screwholes and perhaps pilot holes for nails. If you have a choice, use a cordless drill, so that you don't have to worry about the cable snaking about the workshop. To drill, you simply switch on the power, set the point of the bit on the mark, make sightings to ensure that the bit is square to the face of the item being drilled, and then run the hole through. When you have to put in a lot of screws (see Fig 4), a screwdriver drill attachment is very useful.

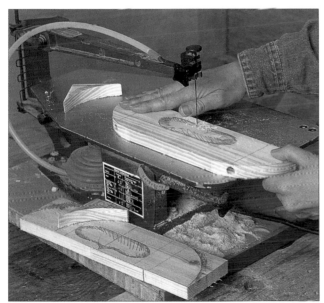

FIG 2

DRILLING HOLES

Use the bench drill press in conjunction with a forstner bit for drilling large holes that need to be precisely placed and worked (see Fig 3). Establish the centre of the hole, fit the appropriate size bit, set the depth stop and clamp the workpiece securely to the drill table. Clamping the workpiece takes a little extra time, but is worth doing because you can locate the hole more accurately, the finish of the hole will be better, and the procedure is safer. Lower the bit to ensure that the point is directly on centre, then switch on the power and run the hole through. If the hole is deep, lift the bit

FIG 3

FIG 4

HAND PLANING

Hand planing is a very satisfying procedure, as long as the plane is sharp and you take your time. I use a smoothing plane for working in the direction of the grain (see Fig 5) along edges and faces. Make sure that the workpiece is secure, turn the brass advancing wheel to set the blade, perform a trial cut to judge whether or not the blade is at the correct depth, and then make the cut. When you are working the edge grain, hold the plane at a slightly skewed angle, with the fingers of your left hand under the sole of the plane to ensure that the plane is square to the face of the wood.

FIG 5

The block plane is perfect for trimming arris (sharp edge) details (see Fig 6) and for tidying up end grain. Adjust the blade so that it makes the lightest of skimming cuts, have a trial on an offcut, and then make the stroke. When you are working end grain, be careful not to run off course and split the grain (see Fig 7).

FIG 6

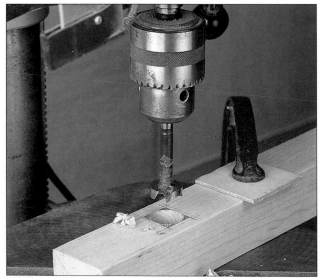

FIG 7

HAND CUTTING A MORTISE

Having used a pencil, rule, set square and perhaps the point of a knife to set out the mortise, move to the bench drill press and use the appropriate size bit to bore out most of the waste (see Fig 8). Be careful not to drill too near the edge of the mortise. Shake the waste from the hole, secure the workpiece in the vice so that the face to be worked is uppermost, and then take a suitable bevel-edge chisel and pare back the hole to the edge of the mortise (see Fig 9). Hold the chisel upright so that you don't undercut the surface or damage the edges. When you are half-way through, turn the wood over and work from the other side.

FIG 8

FIG 9

ROUTING A MORTISE

Depending on the size and position of the mortise, you can use a router to make the cut. You can either use the router as a hand-held tool and plunge down to clear the waste, or for an open-ended mortise (see Fig 10), you can attach the router to its table and run a groove from one end of the workpiece. In this instance, the accuracy of the cuts relates to the setting of the fence and the height of the bit. Always test your settings by routing into an offcut (not a final component). It is best to cut the depth in stages, making several passes that do not overstrain the router. Make sure that you clear the waste after each pass to avoid overheating the bit.

HAND CUTTING A TENON

Begin by marking the shoulder-line (the length of the tenon) with a square and knife, and then mark the depth and width of the tenon with a marking gauge. Remove the waste with a tenon saw: first run a cut down the grain to the waste side of the gauged lines (stop the cut at the shoulder-line) on all four sides of the tenon. Cut across the grain to the waste side of the shoulder-line on all four sides, removing all the waste. Use a chisel to clean up the tenon and trim it to its proper size where necessary.

ROUTING A TENON

If you have a lot of tenons to make (or if you just like using machines), a router set in a table is the ideal tool for the job, as long as your pieces of wood are of a size that can be supported by the table (bigger pieces of wood are best clamped to the bench and routed by hand). All you do is set the fence to the length of the tenon, adjust the router bit to the appropriate height, then hold the workpiece hard against the push-fence and clear the waste with a series of passes (see Fig 11). When the end of the tenon reaches the fence, you turn the workpiece over and re-run the procedure on the other side. If you stop just before the router bit reaches the shoulder-line, you can use a chisel to tidy up.

FIG 10

FIG 11

ROUTING A GROOVE
WITH THE GRAIN

To cut a groove that is 6 mm wide, 4 mm deep and lies 10 mm in from the edge of a board, follow these steps. Attach the router to its table and fit a 6 mm groove cutter. Set the fence to 10 mm. Adjust the cutter so that it stands 2 mm higher than the router table. Switch on the power and push the wood along the fence to cut a groove to a depth of 2 mm (see Fig 12). Switch off the power, and then set the cutter 2 mm higher and re-run the pass to cut the groove to 4 mm.

ROUTING A REBATE ON
THE END OF A BOARD

To cut a rebate that is 10 mm wide and 4 mm deep, follow this procedure. You need a straight cutter that is smaller than the width of the rebate – for example 5 mm. Put the router in the router table and fit the cutter. Set the fence 5 mm back from the rear edge of the cutter, and adjust the cutter height to 2 mm. Switch on the power. Hold the workpiece against the push-fence and make a cut that laps into the end of the board by about 5 mm. Re-run the cut – keeping the end of the board against the fence – in order to cut the full 10 mm width of the rebate. Switch off the power, adjust the cutter so that it stands 4 mm high, and repeat the sequence to complete the cut (see Fig 13).

ROUTING A HOUSING
GROOVE FREEHAND

Clamp the workpiece to the bench. Fit a router cutter that is either the same size or smaller than the width of the groove, and set the depth stop. Clamp a guide strip of wood across the workpiece to run parallel to the groove, so that the cutter will run up the waste side of the drawn line. Set the router down with the base pressed against the guide, switch on the power and wait until the cutter is up to speed, then make the cut. If the cutter is smaller than the groove, shift the guide strip closer and re-run the procedure until the groove is the correct width and depth (see Fig 14).

FIG 12

FIG 13

FIG 14

ROUTING EDGE PROFILES

Cutting an edge profile is one of the easiest routing procedures. Attach the router to its table and fit your chosen cutter – radius (see Fig 16), cove (see Fig 15), Roman or other type. Use one with a pilot or bearing roller-tip. Move the fence so that it is well out of the way. Switch on the power and wait until the router is up to full speed. Now press the workpiece down on the table and run it repeatedly against the cutter. Work with an easy, firm motion so that the cutter enters on the left and exits on the right. Continue until the workpiece rubs up against the pilot or roller-tip, at which point the cutter will cease to cut. If the profiled edge looks burnt, the router cutter might be blunt, or you may be moving too slowly across the wood.

FIG 15

FIG 16

ROUTING WITH A TEMPLATE

A template is used when you want to produce a number of identically shaped components with a smooth routed finish on all the edges. The components first need to be sawn roughly to the shape required, leaving no more than 4–5 mm of waste wood to be removed by the router. Fit a guide brush to the base of the router. Cut a template from sheet plywood, allowing for the collar, and pin it directly to the face of the wood that you want to cut. Switch on the power and wait for the cutter to get up to full speed, then follow the edge of the template to make the cut.

A similar, but more immediate technique for duplicating a component uses the router, a straight cutter with a bearing attached (the bearing can be at the top or bottom of the cutter) and the original finished component, which is used as the template. The procedure is the same as that described above.

CUTTING MITRES WITH A FRAME SAW

The frame saw is an easy way of achieving angled saw cuts. Adjust the saw blade within the frame to your chosen angle – 90°, 45°, 36°, 22.5° or 15° – and lock it in place. Set the depth stop to the chosen depth. Position the workpiece on the saw table, hard up against the fence, and then gently run the saw backwards and forwards to make the cut (see Fig 17).

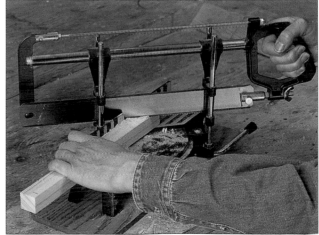
FIG 17

23

NAILING AND PINNING

Look at the workpiece to decide whereabouts the nail or pin is to be sited. If it is near an edge or end, where there is a chance that the wood will split, or you want to ensure that the nail goes in straight, run a pilot hole through with an electric drill, using a bit that is slightly smaller than the diameter of the nail. Set the point of the nail in the hole and use an appropriate size hammer to drive it home. Give it a series of well-placed taps (see Fig 18), all the while watching to make sure that the point of the nail doesn't break through the other side. If it does run off course, use a pair of pliers or a claw hammer to draw it out. If you are using very small pins, which are fiddly to hold and hammer in, use a pair of long-nose pliers to grip the pin as you nail.

FIG 18

SCREWING

You have a choice of using mild steel, stainless-steel, brass or aluminium screws (either cross-headed or slot-headed) with various countersunk or domed heads. Dome-headed screws stand proud of the wood; countersunk screws are set flush with the surface, or held in a brass cup, or hidden by a plug of wood. Screws are driven in with a cross-point or flat screwdriver, either by hand or using an electric drill fitted with a screwdriver bit (see Fig 19). If you use a screwdriver bit in an electric drill, set the slipping clutch mechanism so that the screw is driven in to the correct depth. If the wood is

soft, you can spike a pilot hole with an awl (see Fig 20); if it is hard you can bore a pilot hole with a small drill bit. If you want to cover the screws with a wood plug, you will need a counter-bore bit to drill the pilot hole and the hole for the plug, and a matching plug cutter to cut the plug. I find it is best to practise the entire drilling and screwing operation on a piece of the scrap. Do not use steel screws for oak, because they react with the wood and moisture to leave a stain. Use plated steel, brass or stainless-steel screws instead.

FIG 19

FIG 20

WOODTURNING

If you want to make true round-section items such as chair legs, bowls and platters, the only way to do it is to turn them on a lathe. Buy the highest powered, heaviest lathe that you can afford – one with an expanding chuck and a selection of face plates. Spindles and cylinders are pivoted and turned between the head centre and the tailstock centre (see Fig 21), while bowls and dishes are generally turned on a flat face plate. The best lathes are fitted with a device that allows you to turn large face-plate items on the outboard end of the drive spindle (see Fig 22). You will need various turning tools: a gouge, parting tool, skew chisel and a round-nosed scraper. Lathes can be very dangerous, so always follow the safety instructions.

FIG 21

FIG 22

WHITTLING

All you need for whittling items such as door knobs and catches is a good, sharp knife (not stainless steel). The wood should be a smooth-grained variety. Take the wood in one hand and the knife in the other, and work with a series of tight, paring, thumb-pushing strokes (see Fig 23). The only way to become good at whittling is to get plenty of practice. In the first instance, try working with a piece of lime or basswood.

FIG 23

FIXING HINGES

We use two hinge types: decorative brass hinges that are surface mounted with countersunk screws set flush with the hinge plate, and steel hinges set in a recess and fixed with countersunk steel screws. To recess a hinge, mark round the flap with the point of a fine-bladed knife, use a chisel to chop down to the waste side of the scored line, and finally skim out the waste with a sharp chisel. Work cautiously so that the hinge is a tight push fit in the recess, and take care to control the chisel so that it doesn't lift the surrounding grain. If you are worried about recessing a hinge, then either have several trial runs on scrap wood until you get it right, or opt for hinges that sit flush with the surface. There are a lot of different designs on the market, so you can easily choose a type that suits your needs and skill level. Always obtain screws at the same time as the hinges, to ensure that the countersink is compatible.

SANDING

The sanding or rubbing-down procedure involves using a variety of sandpapers to produce a smooth finish. Use the sandpaper as it is or fold it round a sanding block (see Fig 24), or use an electric sander (see Fig 25). I usually sand several times during a project – when the edges have been sawn, after the glue has cured, and before and after the final finish. I tend to use ordinary glasspaper for the initial rubbing down, and fine-grade aluminium oxide paper when I want to achieve a special finish. Aluminium oxide paper is more expensive than glasspaper, but it lasts much longer. My favourite electric sander is an orbital type which is really good for large, flat surfaces. When you are sanding, work in a ventilated area and wear a dust mask (see page 13).

NATURAL FINISHES

A natural finish literally means that the wood is sanded and then left in its natural state, but the term has also come to mean a surface that has been oiled or waxed. Danish oil and teak oil can be applied with a lint-free cotton cloth or a brush (see Fig 26). You lay on a thin coat, let it dry, wipe it over with the finest grade of sandpaper to remove the "nibs" (the rough texture created by raised wood fibres that are left after the first coat of oil has soaked in) and then apply another thin coat. If you want to soften the surface, you can follow the second rubbing down with wax polish.

For projects that come into direct contact with food, replace teak or Danish oil with a vegetable oil. I use ordinary olive oil wiped on with a cloth (see Fig 27).

FIG 24

FIG 26

FIG 25

FIG 27

PAINTED FINISH

When it comes to painting a solid colour you have a choice between using spirit-based oil paint (see Fig 28) or water-based acrylic paint. Both paints need to be carefully applied with a brush. Though there is very little visual difference between the end results produced by the two types of paint, brushes used for oil paint need to be cleaned with white spirit, while those used for acrylic paint can be cleaned under running water. Currently, I choose paints for their depth and quality of colour, rather than for anything else. As for the side-effects of working with paint, I find that oil fumes tend to make me woozy, while acrylic fumes dry my throat. My advice is to wear a mask to protect you from toxic vapours whichever paint you are using, and as far as possible, to do the painting out in the open.

FIG 28

SPECIAL FINISHES

When using American oak, you can obtain an interesting finish by scouring the grain with a wire brush. I particularly like the feel of a wire-brushed finish, and the rugged surface means that I don't have to worry about my dogs' paws damaging it. The wire brush is rubbed in the direction of the grain (see Fig 29) until the soft areas break down, and the wood is finished with oil.

The candle-smoking technique is fun to do and perfect for covering up a poor-grade wood. Brush the painted surface with oil-based varnish, wait for it to become tacky, and then play the candle flame over the surface (see Fig 30). Always wait for the surface to go tacky (so that it just takes a fingerprint), and always keep the can of varnish and the brushes well away from the candle. This is a procedure that is best managed with a friend's help, in an area well away from the workshop. Practise on an offcut before you start.

FIG 29

FIG 30

KEY TO THE PROJECTS

◇ Ideal beginner's project

◇ Perfect for those who have some experience of woodworking

◇ Ambitious projects, which experienced carpenters will enjoy

Tableware

We all enjoy sitting around a table and sharing a meal with family and friends. But just think how much more fun it would be if you could boast that you had made the tableware. This project involves making two items: oak eggcups that double up as napkin rings, and heart-shaped plywood table mats with their own rack. The designs are somewhat kitsch, but the fact that the shapes and the colours are over the top is part of their appeal, and children will love them too. Also, both eggcups and mats are very practical, and perfect for a young family.

The woodworking techniques are amazingly easy – just a case of drilling large holes and fretting the plywood on the scroll saw. The painting is slightly more difficult and needs to be done with care. When the project is finished, and the items are being used at the breakfast table, don't be surprised to see your children piling the eggcups into stacks and playing with the heart shapes – take it as a sign that they are a success!

Essential Tools

workbench with vice and holdfast, compasses,
pencil, rule, square, bench drill press or electric drill,
45 mm forstner bit, clamps, sanding block, 25 mm and
10 mm paintbrushes, scissors, scroll saw, router and
router table, 5 mm radius cutter, 5 mm and 8 mm
twist bits, pilot-countersink bit, medium-size hammer

OTHER USEFUL TOOLS
cordless screwdriver, power sander, dividers,
marking knife

Tableware

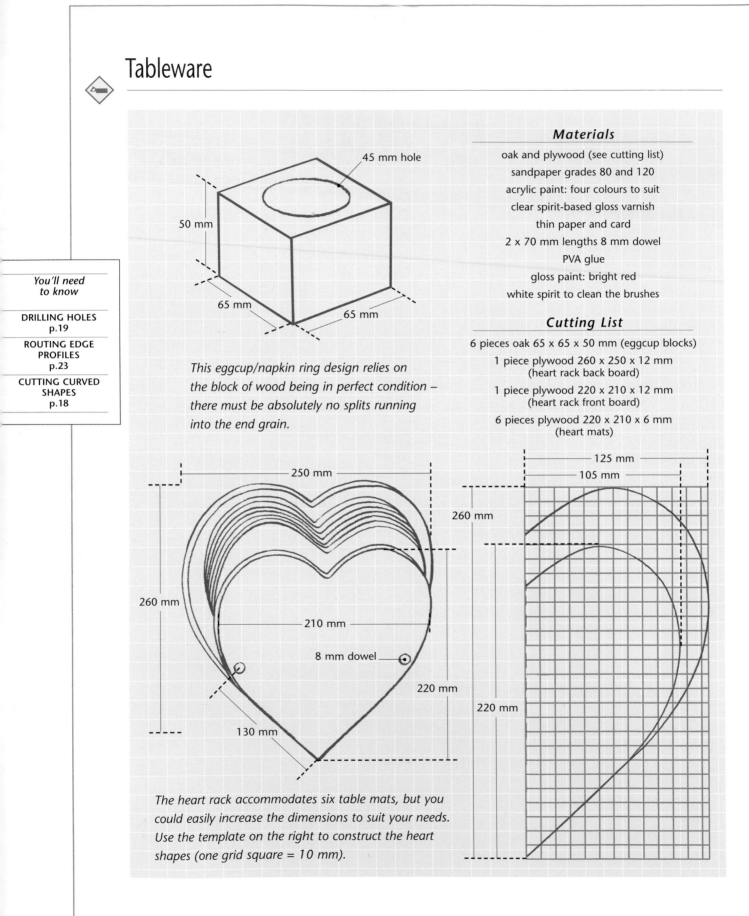

45 mm hole

50 mm

65 mm

65 mm

**You'll need
to know**

DRILLING HOLES
p.19

ROUTING EDGE
PROFILES
p.23

CUTTING CURVED
SHAPES
p.18

Materials

oak and plywood (see cutting list)

sandpaper grades 80 and 120

acrylic paint: four colours to suit

clear spirit-based gloss varnish

thin paper and card

2 x 70 mm lengths 8 mm dowel

PVA glue

gloss paint: bright red

white spirit to clean the brushes

Cutting List

6 pieces oak 65 x 65 x 50 mm (eggcup blocks)

1 piece plywood 260 x 250 x 12 mm
(heart rack back board)

1 piece plywood 220 x 210 x 12 mm
(heart rack front board)

6 pieces plywood 220 x 210 x 6 mm
(heart mats)

*This eggcup/napkin ring design relies on
the block of wood being in perfect condition –
there must be absolutely no splits running
into the end grain.*

250 mm

260 mm

210 mm

8 mm dowel

220 mm

130 mm

125 mm

105 mm

260 mm

220 mm

*The heart rack accommodates six table mats, but you
could easily increase the dimensions to suit your needs.
Use the template on the right to construct the heart
shapes (one grid square = 10 mm).*

EGGCUPS/NAPKIN RINGS

FIG 1

1 Take your prepared oak blocks and check them over to make sure that they are free from cracks. Draw crossed diagonals to establish the position of the centre points (see Fig 1). Do this on both sides of the block.

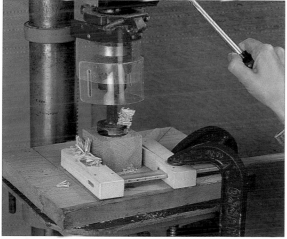

FIG 2

2 Fit the 45 mm forstner bit in the bench drill press. Secure the workpiece with clamps – one to grip the workpiece, another to hold the waste board down on the table, and another clamp to hold the gripping clamp. Run a hole through the 50 mm thickness (see Fig 2). Keep clearing the waste so the bit does not overheat.

TIP

The only way of drilling a smooth-sided, large-diameter hole is to use a forstner bit. They are much more expensive than ordinary bits, but they will last a lot longer. When you bore out the holes, run the bit in little by little, so the waste is removed without overheating the bit.

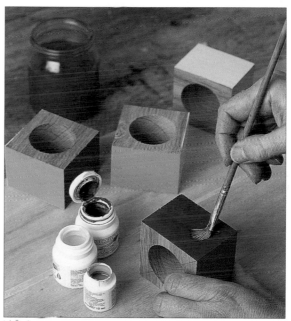

FIG 3

3 Use the graded sandpapers to rub down all the surfaces to a smooth finish. When you are happy with the results, wipe away the mess and move to a clean, dust-free area that you have set aside for painting. Take one block at a time and brush on the acrylic colours – make one side red, another side blue, and so on (see Fig 3). Continue until all the sides of all of the blocks are painted. When the paint is completely dry, use the finest grade of sandpaper to gently rub down the raised hairs of wood. Finally, give all the surfaces a coat of clear gloss varnish.

HEART TABLE MATS

FIG 1

FIG 3

4 Draw the two heart shapes on paper and then transfer to card. Use the card template to draw out the shapes on the plywood (see Fig 1). Mark the shape with a single drawn line, so there is no doubting the line of cut.

6 Attach the router to its table and fit the radius cutter. Set the boards face down on the table and profile the edges so they are nicely rounded (see Fig 3). Do both sides of the heart front and back board that make the rack.

FIG 2

FIG 4

5 Cut out the eight hearts on the scroll saw – two from the 12 mm plywood, and six from the 6 mm. Run a cut straight in and out of the cleft at the top of the heart, and then work from the point back into the cleft (see Fig 2). Saw at a steady, easy pace, all the while making sure that the cut is to the waste side of the drawn line.

7 Draw in the position of the dowel centres on the hearts for the rack. Drill a pair of holes in the front board with the 8 mm twist bit. Hold the two boards together with a length of dowel, and drill the other holes (see Fig 4). Drill out the two hanging holes with the 5 mm twist bit and finish with the pilot-countersink bit.

FIG 5

FIG 6

8 Take the two 70 mm dowels and round over the ends with sandpaper. Set the back and front boards together on the dowels and fix them in place with glue. Use the hammer to nudge the boards about 38 mm apart, so that the dowel ends protrude on the front face (see Fig 5), and wipe away the glue. Check to make sure that the rack holds all six mats comfortably.

9 Wipe away all traces of dust and move to a clean area that you have set aside for painting. Give all surfaces a couple of coats of bright red gloss paint (see Fig 6), so that the hearts look attractively shiny. Finally, when the paint is absolutely dry, rub over the surfaces with the finest grade of sandpaper and give everything a coat of varnish. Sand and varnish again.

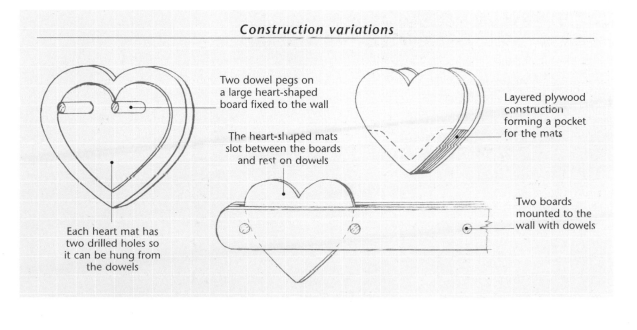

Construction variations

Two dowel pegs on a large heart-shaped board fixed to the wall

The heart-shaped mats slot between the boards and rest on dowels

Each heart mat has two drilled holes so it can be hung from the dowels

Layered plywood construction forming a pocket for the mats

Two boards mounted to the wall with dowels

Kitchen wall rack

The wall rack is a great project for the kitchen. If you have got nowhere to hang your pots and pans, and spoons, slices and spatulas are strewn across the worksurface, transform your life with this really attractive design feature, which stores all the utensils at an easy-to-reach height. And if you are keen on drying herbs, or collecting and displaying antique utensils, the holes at the end of the slats and the brass cuphooks will come in extremely useful for suspending items, using a ribbon if necessary.

The wall rack is very easy to to make – just a small amount of work on the scroll saw, and a bit of drilling. The success of the project relies on the spacing of the slats, which has to be just right, and the finish – you do need to take time with the sanding. The good thing about the design of the rack is its flexibility. For example, if you require a wider rack, all you do is add another vertical runner and lengthen the slats accordingly. Measure the wall space and adjust the overall size of the rack to fit. Check the position of water pipes and power cables before you screw the rack to the wall.

Essential Tools

workbench with vice and holdfast, compasses, pencil,
rule, square, clamp, scroll saw, bench drill press,
10 mm, 5 mm and 3 mm twist bits, electric drill,
screwdriver, sanding block, paintbrush

OTHER USEFUL TOOLS
cordless screwdriver, power sander, marking knife,
block plane

Kitchen wall rack

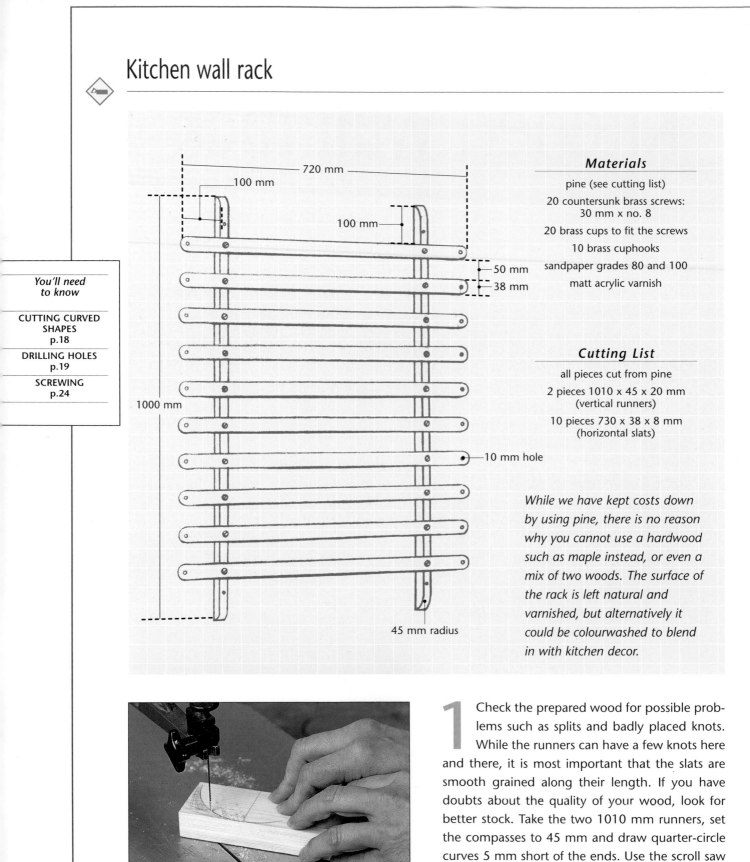

720 mm

100 mm

100 mm

50 mm
38 mm

1000 mm

10 mm hole

45 mm radius

Materials

pine (see cutting list)

20 countersunk brass screws:
30 mm x no. 8

20 brass cups to fit the screws

10 brass cuphooks

sandpaper grades 80 and 100

matt acrylic varnish

Cutting List

all pieces cut from pine

2 pieces 1010 x 45 x 20 mm
(vertical runners)

10 pieces 730 x 38 x 8 mm
(horizontal slats)

While we have kept costs down by using pine, there is no reason why you cannot use a hardwood such as maple instead, or even a mix of two woods. The surface of the rack is left natural and varnished, but alternatively it could be colourwashed to blend in with kitchen decor.

FIG 1

1 Check the prepared wood for possible problems such as splits and badly placed knots. While the runners can have a few knots here and there, it is most important that the slats are smooth grained along their length. If you have doubts about the quality of your wood, look for better stock. Take the two 1010 mm runners, set the compasses to 45 mm and draw quarter-circle curves 5 mm short of the ends. Use the scroll saw to cut the ends to shape (see Fig 1).

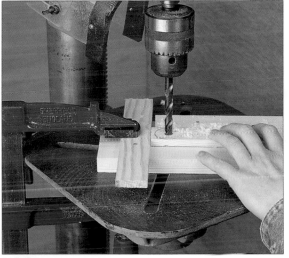

FIG 2

2 Take the slats and use the compasses to set out circles 35 mm in diameter on the ends. Have the circles set back 5 mm from the ends, so that the slats all finish up at 720 mm long. On the bench drill press, run 10 mm holes through the centre points (see Fig 2).

FIG 3

FIG 4

3 Cut the ends of the slats to shape on the scroll saw (see Fig 3). Do your best to cut slightly to the waste side of the drawn line, so that the curve is true. If you fit a new blade and work at an easy pace, the sawn edges will hardly need sanding. Make sure the blade is fitted so the teeth point down towards the table.

4 Mark guidelines on the runners, spacing the slats 50 mm apart. For each screw, drill 5 mm holes through the slats and 3 mm pilot holes into the runners. Fix the slats with the screws and cups (see Fig 4). Sand all the surfaces, fit the cuphooks, and varnish the whole wall rack. The end grain might need a couple of coats.

Tea tray

The styles of the 1950s do not excite everyone, but there is something about the simplicity of the period that is most appealing. Designers of the time experimented with smooth curves, new materials such as plastics, and lots of primary colours, making many of the household items appear quite daring. This little 1950s-style tray is also quite different to the ornate mahogany and brass of earlier times, instead using a sheet of plywood with simple strip wood handles. We have chosen white and red enamel paint – which would have been just right for the red-and-white kitchens of the 1950s – but you may prefer to select an alternative colour scheme.

   The making procedures are very easy. All the parts are fretted out on the scroll saw, the individual components are painted, and then the tray is put together with brass screws. What could be easier? That said, the success of the project relies on the sawn lines being crisp and clean, and the paint finish being smooth and free from runs and dribbles. If you have doubts about your painting skills, practise on a piece of scrap wood first.

Essential Tools

workbench with vice, compasses, pencil, rule,
square, scroll saw, sanding block, paintbrush, electric
drill, 3 mm twist bit,
pilot-countersink bit, screwdriver

OTHER USEFUL TOOLS
cordless screwdriver, power sander, dividers,
marking knife, block plane

Tea tray

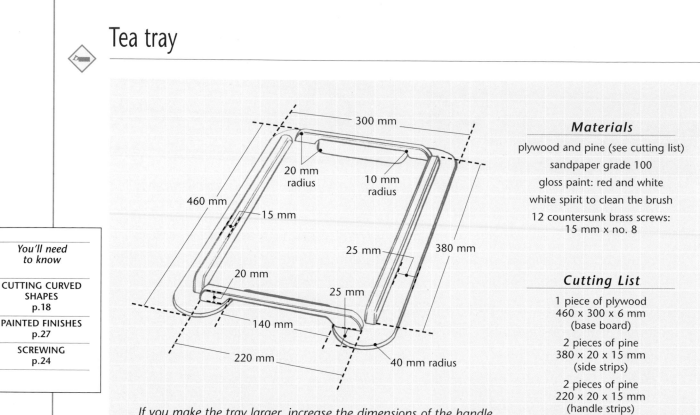

300 mm
20 mm radius
10 mm radius
460 mm
15 mm
25 mm
380 mm
20 mm
25 mm
140 mm
220 mm
40 mm radius

Materials

plywood and pine (see cutting list)

sandpaper grade 100

gloss paint: red and white

white spirit to clean the brush

12 countersunk brass screws:
15 mm x no. 8

Cutting List

1 piece of plywood
460 x 300 x 6 mm
(base board)

2 pieces of pine
380 x 20 x 15 mm
(side strips)

2 pieces of pine
220 x 20 x 15 mm
(handle strips)

*If you make the tray larger, increase the dimensions of the handle
strips so that they are strong enough to carry a heavier weight.*

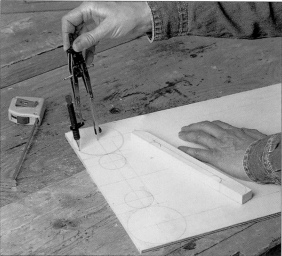

FIG 1

FIG 2

1 Measure 40 mm along from each end of the base board, rule a line across and draw the large circles (40 mm radius) and the smaller circles (20 mm radius). Set out the handles with radii of 10 mm and 20 mm (see Fig 1).

2 Check against the working drawing to ensure that all is correct, and then fret out the parts on the scroll saw (base, handles and side strips). The line of cut must be slightly to the waste side of the drawn line (see Fig 2).

TIPS

The painting is tricky – to achieve a good finish, lay the paint on as two or more thin coats. Wipe away the dust, lay on the first coat and let it dry, sand slightly, lay on another coat, and so on until you have a high-shine finish.

4 Mark out the position of the side and handle strips on the base board and drill 3 mm pilot holes through the base and about 5 mm into the strips. Countersink the base holes on what will be the underside of the tray, and finally screw the strips in place (see Fig 4).

FIG 3

3 Sand the sawn faces to a slightly round-edged finish. Paint the parts with the gloss paint – red for the side and handle strips and white for both sides of the base. When the paint is completely dry, repeat the rubbing down with the finest grade of sandpaper (see Fig 3), and lay on another thin coat of paint.

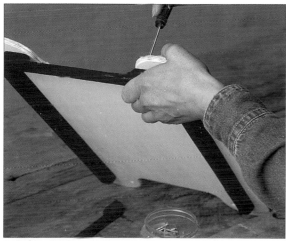

FIG 4

Construction variations

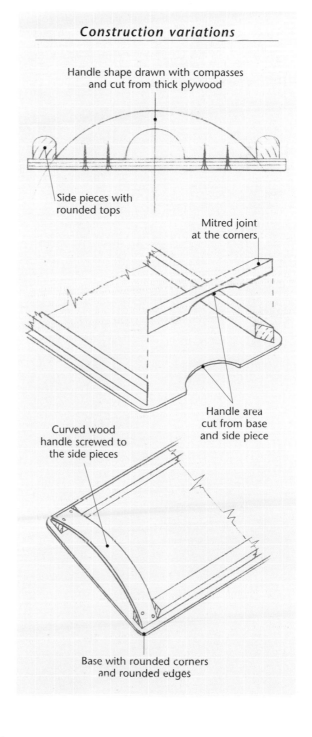

Handle shape drawn with compasses and cut from thick plywood

Side pieces with rounded tops

Mitred joint at the corners

Handle area cut from base and side piece

Curved wood handle screwed to the side pieces

Base with rounded corners and rounded edges

Consul shelf

This project looks to the painted folk art woodwork that was made in America in the nineteenth century by the German settlers in Pennsylvania. It was characterized by very simple construction, using lots of nails, and was painted either with brightly coloured motifs and designs, or given an overall texture to fool the eye into believing that it was made from an exotic wood.

This particular little shelf is decorated by a technique known as candle marbling or smoking. The wood is painted with a base colour, usually red, blue or green, and then, when the paint is dry, the surface is brushed with spirit-based varnish, left until it is tacky, and finally the tip of the flame of a lighted candle is played over the surface. The black carbon from the flame bleeds into the varnish to create a shimmering, opalescent blue-black effect, a bit like the bloom on a fresh black plum.

The shelf's construction is very basic. The three components are fretted out on the scroll saw and then simply fixed with screws that run down from the top and in from the back. The only slightly more ornate piece of woodwork is the cyma curve bracket that supports the shelf.

Essential Tools

workbench with vice, compass, pencil, rule, square, scroll saw, router and router table, 6.3 mm radius cutter, sanding block, hand drill, 3 mm twist bit, pilot-countersink bit, screwdriver, 2 paintbrushes

OTHER USEFUL TOOLS
cordless screwdriver, power sander, electric drill, dividers, marking knife, block plane, tenon saw

Consul shelf

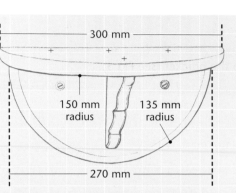

The consul shelf is screwed together:
2 screws fix the back to the bracket,
3 screws fix the shelf to the back and
1 screw fixes the shelf to the bracket.
Below: template for the bracket.

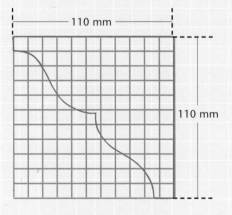

**You'll need
to know**

CUTTING CURVED
SHAPES
p.18

ROUTING EDGE
PROFILES
p.23

SPECIAL FINISHES
p.27

Materials

pine (see cutting list)

sandpaper grades 80 and 150

6 countersunk steel screws: 30 mm x no. 8

matt, spirit-based tile paint: red

spirit-based clear varnish

white spirit to clean the brushes

large candle

Cutting List

all pieces cut from pine

1 piece 300 x 160 x 18 mm (shelf board)

1 piece 270 x 140 x 18 mm (back board)

1 piece 110 x 110 x 18 mm (bracket board)

FIG 1

1 Use the compasses to set out the shelf board at a radius of 150 mm, and the back board at 135 mm. Transfer the shape of the cyma curve to the bracket board (see Fig 1).

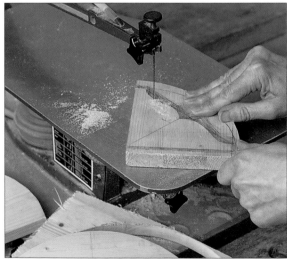

FIG 2

2 Fret out the three component parts on the scroll saw – the half-circle of the shelf board to a finished diameter of 150 mm, the half-circle back board to a diameter of 270 mm, and the right-angled cyma-curve bracket to measure 110 mm x 110 mm (see Fig 2).

FIG 3

3 Fit the radius cutter in the router and attach the router to its table. Cut radius curves on the underside of the shelf and on the front of the back board (see Fig 3).

FIG 4

4 Use the sanding block and fine-grade sandpaper to rub down everything to a smooth finish. Pay particular attention to the edge of the shelf and the sawn edges of the cyma curve (see Fig 4). Drill 3 mm pilot holes for the screws and countersink with the pilot-countersink bit.

FIG 5

5 Have a trial fitting to make sure that everything is correct, and then screw the pieces together. The screws run through the back board into the bracket, and through the shelf board into the top edge of the back board and into the bracket (see Fig 5).

FIG 6

6 Paint the shelf red. When the paint is dry, lay on a thin coat of varnish. When the varnish is tacky and almost dry, light the candle and play the tip of the flame over the surface to create the marbled effect (see Fig 6). Be careful not to overdo the smoking, especially at the edges, or it will obliterate the red colour. Finally, give the shelf a second coat of varnish.

TIP

Caution – keep the varnish and white spirit away from the lighted candle, because both are highly flammable. The varnished surface must be tacky before you start the candle work, or you won't achieve the correct result.

Colonial wall shelf

The houses of early settlers in America were filled with all manner of shelves. There were consul shelves for candles, shelves for bags and pouches, shelves for storing dry goods, and so on. All were put together with the minimum of joints, and charmingly decorated in a naïve style. The shelf in this project beautifully recreates the work of the New England craftsmen, who were masters of compass work and the cyma curve.

The low-tech housing groove and glued construction make the shelf a great project for beginners who have a relatively limited tool kit. Pine is used throughout, making it economical to build. The highly fretted edges turn it into a very decorative piece, so it would be perfect for a living room display shelf. The side boards are cleverly designed so that the symmetrical shapes are easy to achieve by eye and with compasses. All you do is draw the design on one side of the centre-line and then trace it off and flip it over to the other side. Make sure that the fretted edges of the side boards are free from knots and splits, especially the curves lying just in front of the shelves.

Essential Tools

workbench with vice and holdfast, compasses,
pencil, rule, square, scroll saw, router and router table,
13 mm groove cutter, clamps, knife, sanding block,
paintbrush, screwdriver

OTHER USEFUL TOOLS
cordless screwdriver, power sander, marking knife,
block plane

Colonial wall shelf

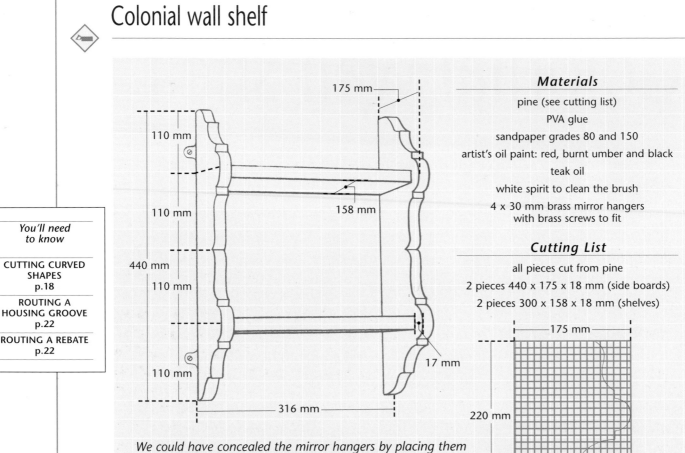

175 mm

110 mm

158 mm

110 mm

440 mm

110 mm

110 mm

110 mm

17 mm

316 mm

Materials

pine (see cutting list)

PVA glue

sandpaper grades 80 and 150

artist's oil paint: red, burnt umber and black

teak oil

white spirit to clean the brush

4 x 30 mm brass mirror hangers
with brass screws to fit

Cutting List

all pieces cut from pine

2 pieces 440 x 175 x 18 mm (side boards)

2 pieces 300 x 158 x 18 mm (shelves)

175 mm

220 mm

We could have concealed the mirror hangers by placing them on the inside, but traditonally hangers were set as "ears", so they become a decorative detail, and we have followed suit.

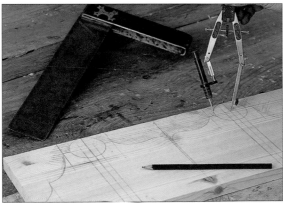

FIG 1

FIG 2

1 Arrange the two 440 mm sides so that the best edges are facing outwards. Divide into four equal pieces and use the square, rule and compasses to set out the design (see Fig 1).

2 Using the scroll saw, run a cut along the centre-line, and then back out of the kerf (saw cut). Fret out the design, finishing in the cleft (see Fig 2). Do this for both side boards.

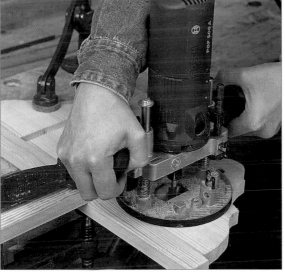

FIG 3

FIG 4

3 Use the router and 13 mm groove cutter to cut the housing grooves. Clamp a side board to the bench, and with waste strips in place, adjust the position of the guide to ensure that the router bit is perfectly on course. Set the depth guide to 10 mm. Finally, switch on the power, hold the router base plate hard up against the guide strip, check that the flex is clear, and cut the housing groove (see Fig 3).

4 Mount the router on the router table. Set the fence to 10 mm, and cut shoulders on the shelf ends (see Fig 4). Use the knife to whittle the shoulders to fit the stopped ends of the housing grooves. Glue and clamp up. Sand to a smooth finish. Mix a little of the red, black and burnt umber paint into the teak oil, and brush on one or more coats. Screw the mirror hangers to the back edges of the side boards.

Construction variations

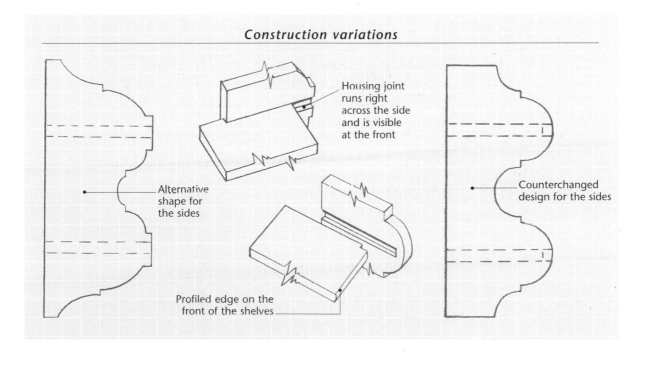

Alternative shape for the sides

Housing joint runs right across the side and is visible at the front

Profiled edge on the front of the shelves

Counterchanged design for the sides

Arts and Crafts mirror

The design of this mirror pays homage to Arts and Crafts designers such as Gustav Stickley and Ernest Gimson with its use of proportion, very slender through-tenons, the way the horizontal members extend beyond the limits of the frame, and the use of dowels to hold the joints together. However, although an Arts and Crafts form will happily blend into most homes, an altogether lighter feel – both in colour and proportions – is perhaps more consistent with modern styles. So, instead of using thick-section oak, we have opted for using a much thinner section of straight-grained pine.

Made from pine throughout, with dowels standing proud and the back rebated to take the mirror glass, this is quite a challenging project. The tricky part is cutting the mortises through the thickness of the wood: you will be cutting a mortise 8 mm wide through a 20 mm piece of pine, with only a 6 mm thickness of wood at either side of the mortise. It will test your skills! If you are not sure whether your woodworking expertise or your tools are up to it, have a trial run on scrap wood beforehand.

Essential Tools

workbench with vice and holdfast, compasses, pencil, rule, square, mortise gauge, clamps, bench drill press, 6 mm and 12 mm forstner bits, mallet, 6 mm and 20 mm bevel-edge chisels, marking knife, router and router table, penknife, 10 mm groove cutter, block plane, small hammer, sanding block, screwdriver

OTHER USEFUL TOOLS
power sander

Arts and Crafts mirror

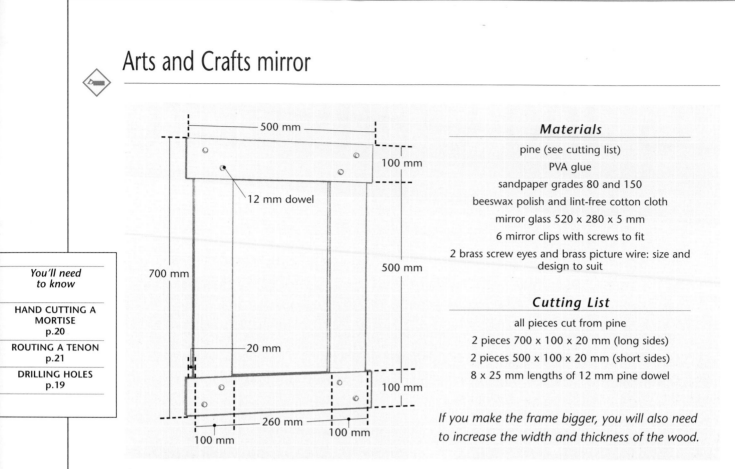

12 mm dowel

500 mm

100 mm

700 mm

500 mm

20 mm

260 mm

100 mm

100 mm

100 mm

Materials

pine (see cutting list)

PVA glue

sandpaper grades 80 and 150

beeswax polish and lint-free cotton cloth

mirror glass 520 x 280 x 5 mm

6 mirror clips with screws to fit

2 brass screw eyes and brass picture wire: size and
design to suit

Cutting List

all pieces cut from pine

2 pieces 700 x 100 x 20 mm (long sides)

2 pieces 500 x 100 x 20 mm (short sides)

8 x 25 mm lengths of 12 mm pine dowel

*If you make the frame bigger, you will also need
to increase the width and thickness of the wood.*

FIG 1

FIG 2

1 Take the two 500 mm lengths of wood and use the square to position the mortises 20 mm along from the ends. Set the spurs of the mortise gauge to 8 mm apart, and score the lines so that they are centred on the 20 mm thickness of wood (see Fig 1). Do this on opposite edges, and on both ends of the wood.

2 Bore through all the mortises with the bench drill press and 6 mm bit, and then use the mallet and bevel-edge chisels to pare the mortises to a smooth, true finish (see Fig 2). Work from both sides of the mortise to keep the edges clean. Don't damage the ends of the holes by levering the tool against the wood.

FIG 3

3 Use the square, marking knife and gauge to set out the 100 mm-long tenons. Attach the router to its table, fit the 10 mm groove cutter in the router, set the fence to 100 mm and the depth of cut to 6 mm. Make a series of passes to cut away the waste (see Fig 3). Re-run this procedure on both sides and both ends, so that you finish up with 8 mm-thick tenons.

FIG 4

4 Reset the fence to 10 mm and run the rebates for the mirror on the inside back edges of the frame. Put the frame components together and use the 12 mm bit to bore the dowel holes through the joints. Check for squareness and overall good fit (see Fig 4), and use the block plane to tidy up the end grain.

FIG 5

5 Fit the frame together, dribble glue in the drilled holes, and tap the dowels home with the hammer (see Fig 5). Leave the dowels standing proud on the front face of the frame. When the glue is completely dry, use the chisel to remove any runs and to trim the edges of the dowels to a slightly round-edged finish. Check that all rebated corners are free from blobs of glue. Use the graded sandpapers to rub the frame to a smooth finish. Finally, wipe away the dust, burnish the frame with the beeswax, fit the mirror glass and screw in the clips to hold it in place, and fix the screw eyes and the hanging wire.

TIP

To be certain that the mirror glass will fit the frame really well, it is best to take the frame to a glazier so it can be measured and the glass cut to fit exactly. Make sure that the glass is properly wrapped and protected before you take it away.

Studio shelf system

This project covers that most basic of items – a simple shelf. For ease of making, it takes a bit of beating – there are no joints to cut, it is just made up of six planks and a handful of screws and dowels. The design is so well considered and cheap to make that you could easily put together a batch of units. As the shelves are fixed directly to the wall with screws through the back boards, they can be removed easily and taken with you when you move house. Simple to make and trouble-free to fit – the perfect shelves!

Made of pine throughout, the construction is wonderfully straightforward. Instead of having the screws running into the end grain (which technically is a bad idea because the threads tend to pull out), they run down through pilot holes and into dowels set across the grain. The dowels are stained black, and the screwheads are covered with glued plugs. When you are driving the screws home, be careful not to over-tighten them to the extent that you expand the dowels and split the wood. Arrange the dowels so that the grain runs at right angles to the screw.

Essential Tools

workbench with vice and holdfast, compasses, pencil, rule, square, block plane, hammer, clamps, bench drill press, 12 mm twist bit, large bevel-edge knife, 7 mm counter-bore bit with a plug cutter to match, screwdriver, sanding block, paintbrush

OTHER USEFUL TOOLS
cordless screwdriver, power sander, marking knife

Studio shelf system

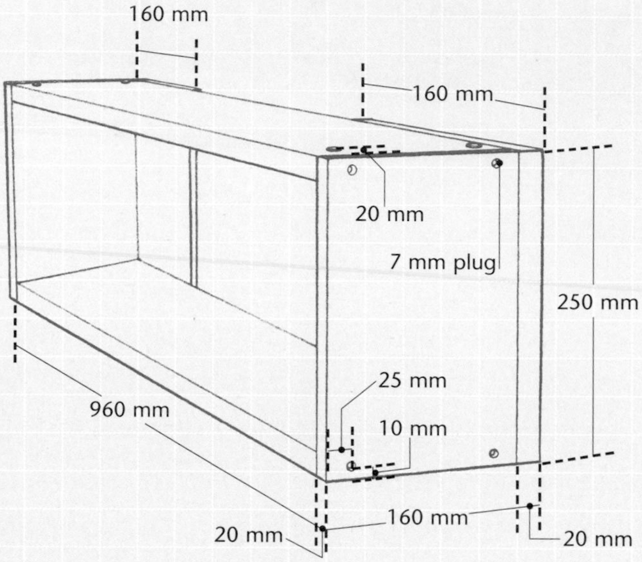

160 mm
160 mm
20 mm
7 mm plug
250 mm
25 mm
960 mm
10 mm
160 mm
20 mm
20 mm

If you like the design of the shelf system but would prefer not to use dowels, see the Adjustable Porch Chair on page 130 for an alternative method of fixing, using hex-head fasteners.

Materials

pine (see cutting list)
wood offcuts for the drilling jig
6 nails for the jig: size to suit
200 mm length of 12 mm dowel
22 countersunk steel screws: 30 mm x no. 8
sandpaper grades 150 to 300
black felt-tip spirit marker
PVA glue
spirit-based matt varnish
white spirit to clean brush

Cutting List

all pieces cut from pine
2 pieces 960 x 160 x 20 mm (shelf boards)
2 pieces 250 x 160 x 20 mm (end boards)
2 pieces 250 x 160 x 20 mm (back boards)

You'll need to know

HAND PLANING p.20
DRILLING HOLES p.19
SCREWING p.24

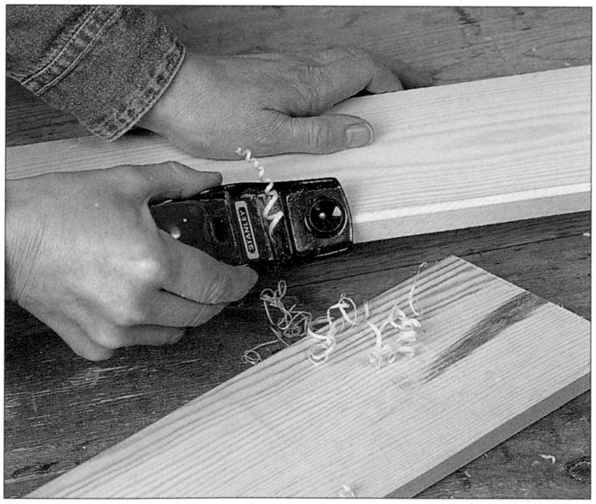
FIG 1

1 Take all six prepared boards (cut to size and planed) and check them over to make sure that they are in good condition, with no warps, splits or badly placed knots. Use the block plane to bring the ends to a good finish and to bevel all the edges slightly (see Fig 1).

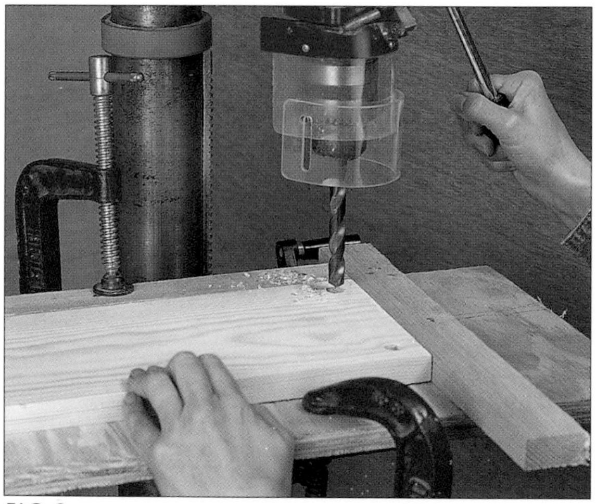
FIG 2

2 Use the hammer, nails and offcuts to build a jig (a device for holding a component during construction) to contain one end of a shelf board. Put a shelf in the jig and clamp it to the table of the bench drill press so the 12 mm bit is in position. Bore out the dowel holes (see Fig 2).

FIG 3

3 Use a rule and pencil to mark off 23 mm intervals on the 12 mm dowel. Set the knife on the mark, and roll the dowel to cut it through (see Fig 3). Note how the wide bevel on the knife gives the dowel a rounded end.

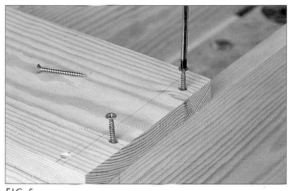

FIG 5

5 Use the counter-bore bit to drill holes through the end boards and back boards. Drive the screws home so that their heads are about 5 mm below the surface (see Fig 5 – shows back board being screwed to shelf).

FIG 4

4 Sand the dowel ends to a slightly domed finish. Stain the ends with the felt-tip (see Fig 4). Push the dowels into the holes in the ends of the shelves (they will stand slightly proud).

FIG 6

6 Cut plugs from a scrap of pine and glue them in place to cover the screws. Finally, sand the entire shelf system to a good finish and brush on a coat of varnish (see Fig 6).

Construction variations

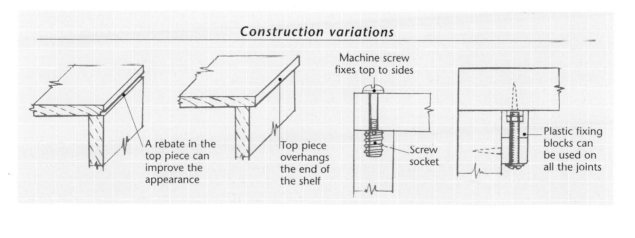

A rebate in the top piece can improve the appearance

Top piece overhangs the end of the shelf

Machine screw fixes top to sides

Screw socket

Plastic fixing blocks can be used on all the joints

Waste bin

This is the perfect bin for the design-conscious home. Get rid of your creaky woven baskets and plastic tubs left over from the 1970s – now you can have a bin that looks as if it belongs in the twenty-first century. This bin will also look good in a home office, or perhaps in the children's room.

Made of top-quality birch plywood throughout, this is one of the easiest projects in the book. The holes must be cut very carefully, and the five boards need to be prepared, glued and pinned together, but apart from that, the construction is amazingly straightforward. The design is also very flexible, so you can choose to change the pattern of drilled holes, or go for a fretted design rather than have holes, or paint the bin in a bright primary colour instead of the natural finish. Do not be tempted to cut costs by using one of the soft-centred plywoods (those originating from Malaysia), because they are of inferior quality. You must use best-quality birch plywood. Ask your supplier for advice if you are not sure what to buy.

Essential Tools
---

workbench with vice, pencil, rule, square, awl,
bench drill press, 25 mm and 40 mm forstner bits,
clamps, power sander, pin hammer, sanding block,
paintbrush

OTHER USEFUL TOOLS
marking knife

Waste bin

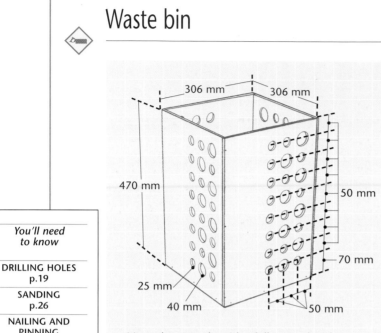

Note the way the sides follow each other so that you only see one edge on each side.

Materials

birch plywood (see cutting list)

masking tape

sandpaper grades 100 and 150

PVA glue

24 x 12 mm steel pins

teak oil

Cutting List

all pieces cut from birch plywood

4 pieces 470 x 300 x 6 mm (sides)

1 piece 294 x 294 x 12 mm (base)

FIG 1

1 Take one of the side boards and use the rule and square to draw out a 50 x 50 mm grid (see Fig 1). Double-check the measurements to make sure that the grid is accurate.

FIG 2

2 Take the four boards that make up the sides and sandwich them together, with the gridded board on top of the stack. Strap them up with masking tape (see Fig 2). Study our design, decide on the pattern of holes you want, and spike in the centre points with the awl.

FIG 3

3 Fit one or other of the forstner bits in the bench drill press, put a waste board on the drill table, and set to work boring the pattern of holes (see Fig 3). To ensure that each hole is cleanly worked, centre the bit on the spiked point, and then clamp the workpiece in place.

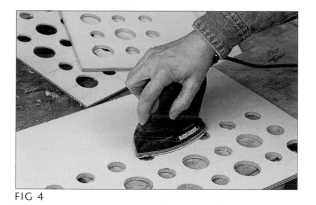

FIG 4

4 When you have bored all the holes, remove the masking tape, and use the sander to rub down the surfaces to a smooth finish (see Fig 4). Be careful not to blur the edges.

FIG 5

5 Fold a piece of fine-grade sandpaper and use it to wipe round the cut edges of the drilled holes (see Fig 5). Continue until the edges are smooth to the touch.

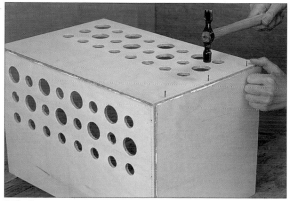

FIG 6

6 Sand down the edges of the base board and glue and pin the sides in place (see Fig 6). Don't let the pins run off course and split the plywood. Finally, sand the bin to a smooth finish and wipe on a coat of teak oil.

TIP

If you are worried about your ability to knock the pins into the edge of the thin plywood, then either ask a friend to help you align the pins, or drill pilot holes with a hand drill and a fine bit.

Construction variations

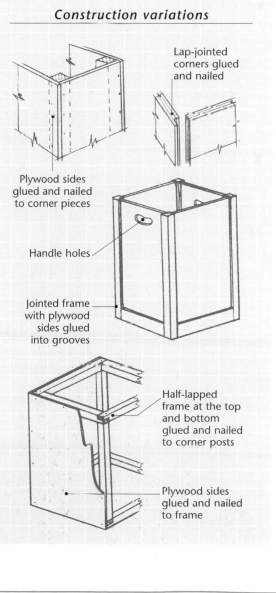

Lap-jointed corners glued and nailed

Plywood sides glued and nailed to corner pieces

Handle holes

Jointed frame with plywood sides glued into grooves

Half-lapped frame at the top and bottom glued and nailed to corner posts

Plywood sides glued and nailed to frame

Child's stool

This beautiful stool was inspired by a stool that my granny had in her country kitchen. When grandad had a few drops of paint left over from another job, the stool was painted. One time it was chicken-shed red, and then garden-gate green, but mostly – I don't know why – it was a vivid yellow. My grandparents used it as a footstool, for standing on to reach high cupboards, and for any number of other tasks, but mostly it was my own special seat. You too may find that the stool fulfils a number of roles.

Even if you are the newest of new weekend carpenters, you will be able to manage the construction process easily. Made from 20 mm-thick pine boards throughout, the components are fretted out on the scroll saw. The splayed legs are housed in grooves cut on the inside face of the two apron boards, and the stool is held together with screws. We have painted it yellow, but other bright colours also work well, such as fire-engine red or electric blue. You could also paint each part in a different colour.

Essential Tools

workbench with vice and holdfast, compasses, pencil, rule, square, bevel gauge, scroll saw, bench drill press or electric drill, 10 mm and 5 mm twist bits, tenon saw, 16 mm bevel-edge chisel, block plane, sanding block, pilot-countersink bit, screwdriver, paintbrush

OTHER USEFUL TOOLS
cordless screwdriver, power sander, dividers, marking knife

Child's stool

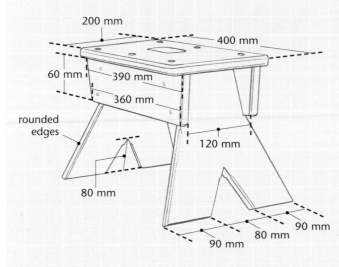

200 mm
400 mm
60 mm
390 mm
360 mm
rounded edges
120 mm
80 mm
90 mm
80 mm
90 mm

The hole in the centre of the seat (detail shown right), which doubles as a handle, must be large enough to ensure that a child cannot get a leg stuck in it.

Materials

pine (see cutting list)
sandpaper grades 80 and 150
12 countersunk steel screws: 30 mm x no. 8
gloss paint: yellow
white spirit to clean the brush

Cutting List

all pieces cut from pine
1 piece 400 x 200 x 18 mm (seat board)
2 pieces 390 x 60 x 18 mm (apron boards)
2 pieces 260 x 260 x 18 mm (leg boards)

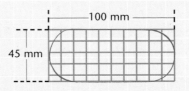

100 mm
45 mm

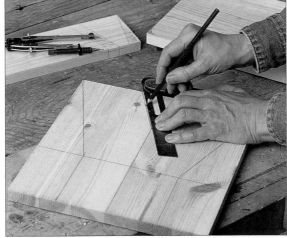

FIG 1

FIG 2

1 Check the prepared boards for possible problems such as splits and badly placed knots. Use the square and bevel gauge to carefully set out the design. When you come to the leg boards, start by drawing a centre-line, and then use the line as a reference point for all the subsequent measurements (see Fig 1).

2 Use the scroll saw to cut out the component parts. Work at a steady, controlled pace, making sure that the line of cut is slightly to the waste side of the drawn line (see Fig 2). If you feel the blade running off course, or it sags, or the cut edge of the wood goes brown and shiny, the blade probably needs replacing.

FIG 3

3 Drill a pilot hole through the seat with the 10 mm twist bit, pass one end of the scroll saw blade through the hole, refit the blade and tension it until it "pings". Cut along the marked line until the waste drops clear (see Fig 3).

TIP

When using a chisel to cut a housing groove, make sure that the chisel is slightly narrower than the finished width of the groove.

FIG 4

4 To create the housing groove on the apron boards, make two cuts with the tenon saw (at 20 mm from the end, slanting to 60 mm from the end; with a parallel 18 mm away, 5 mm deep). Clear the waste with the chisel (see Fig 4).

FIG 5

5 Use the block plane to work all the on-view edges to a slightly rounded finish (as shown in Figs 4 and 6). With the chisel and sandpaper, adjust the sides of the leg boards so that they meet the apron boards for a tight push-fit (see Fig 5). Pencil-label the parts so that the joints are cut to a paired fit.

FIG 6

6 Drill pilot holes with the 5 mm bit, followed by the pilot-countersink bit. Screw the apron boards to the legs and the seat board to the top edge of the aprons, countersinking all the screws. Rub down with the finest grade of sandpaper, wipe up all the dust, and give the stool a coat of yellow gloss paint (see Fig 6). Re-run the procedure for a high-shine finish.

Turned fruit bowl

Fruit always makes an attractive display while it is waiting to be eaten, particularly when it is contained in a beautiful bowl. Wooden bowls look especially appealing, and as a natural material, they complement the fruit perfectly. And what could be better than using a fruit bowl that you have made yourself? Just think of the kudos when your family and friends see the evidence of your talents – you can expect some orders for gifts.

There is no need to get involved in the expensive and wearisome business of searching around for a suitable lump of wood. The good thing about this project is that the bowl is made from straight-grained American oak, and the blank (form for the bowl) is built up in laminated slices cut from a prepared board. The laminating procedure is a bit messy and time-consuming, but on the other hand it means that you do not have to worry about loose knots or splits, or the wood warping out of shape.

—— Essential Tools ——

workbench with vice, compasses, pencil, rule,
scroll saw, 4 long-reach sash or G-clamps, good-size
lathe with a 150 mm-diameter face plate and the
capacity to turn a blank bigger than 250 mm in
diameter, screwdriver, set of turning tools to include
a large gouge and a round-nosed scraper, tailstock
drill chuck to fit your lathe, full-face respirator or
dust mask and goggles, ear defenders, 50 mm
forstner bit, sanding block

OTHER USEFUL TOOLS
cordless screwdriver, power sander, dividers

Turned fruit bowl

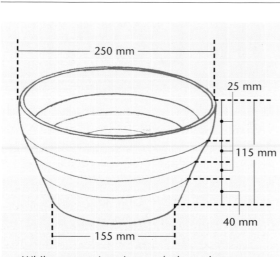

While we use American oak throughout, you could substitute two different-coloured woods to achieve a counterbalanced colour effect, for added interest.

Materials

American oak (see cutting list)
PVA glue
countersunk steel screws to fit lathe face plate
sandpaper grades 100 to 300
vegetable oil
lint-free cotton cloth to apply the vegetable oil

Cutting List

all pieces cut from American oak
1 piece 250 x 250 x 40 mm (base slab)
3 pieces 250 x 250 x 25 mm (top slabs)

You'll need to know

CUTTING CURVES
p.18

WOODTURNING
p.25

NATURAL FINISHES
p.26

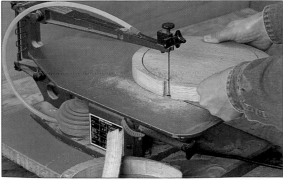

FIG 1

1 Take your planed wood and use the compasses, set at a radius of 125 mm, to set out the four 250 mm-diameter discs. Cut out the discs on the scroll saw (see Fig 1).

FIG 2

2 Smear a generous amount of PVA glue on mating faces, set the wood together in a stack, with all the edges more or less aligned, and clamp up (see Fig 2). Don't worry about the dribbles of glue. Leave for at least 24 hours and then remove the clamps.

FIG 3

3 Set the lathe face plate directly over the centre point of the wood and fix with three or more steel screws (see Fig 3). It is important that the wood is centred and the whole thing is secure. Do not use soft brass or aluminium screws instead of steel, and do not be tempted to curtail the drying time for the glue in step 2.

FIG 4

4 Mount the whole thing on the lathe and set the tool rest just below the centre of spin (see Fig 4). Turn the wood over by hand to make sure that the tool rest is clear.

TIP

Woodturning is potentially dangerous. Put on protective gear and ensure that clothing does not present a hazard.

FIG 5

5 First, use the large gouge to turn the wood to a smooth cylinder 250 mm in diameter, and then turn the cylinder to the shape of the outside of the bowl (see Fig 5). Keep resetting the rest so that it is near the workpiece.

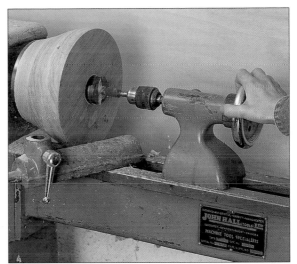

FIG 6

6 Remove the tool rest and fit the 50 mm forstner bit in the tailstock chuck. Slowly advance the tailstock to bore a pilot hole to a depth of about 90 mm, so that it stops about 25 mm short of the bowl bottom (see Fig 6). Keep withdrawing the bit to remove the waste.

FIG 7

7 Move the tool rest so that it is over the bed and very cautiously use the gouge, followed by the scraper, to turn out the centre of the bowl (see Fig 7). Work until you reach the bottom of the drilled pilot hole. When you are pleased with the profile, rub down the bowl with sandpaper and burnish it with vegetable oil.

Kitchen workboards

It is really good to see family and friends using small items that I have made with my own two hands. One day I was looking at a couple of pieces of apple wood and wondering what to make with them, and came up with the idea of kitchen workboards. Not so long afterwards, the boards were out on the table being used for cutting bread and cheese. These boards are not particularly special, in fact they are rather humble, but the warm feeling I get when I see them in use is due to the pleasure of making them, and the knowledge that they are going to be in service for years to come.

Both boards are made from apple wood turned on the lathe. One is decorated by pyrography (branding with a hot iron), while the other is chip carved. Pyrography is very easy: you simply heat the iron and press it into the wood. The chip-carved design is just as straightforward – lots of little boat-shaped knife cuts make a stylized ear of wheat design that is really appropriate for a breadboard. Practise the technique on scrap wood first.

Essential Tools

workbench with vice and holdfast, compass, pencil, rule, scroll saw, lathe with a bowl-turning option and a large face plate, set of turning tools to include a skew chisel, gouge and a round-nosed scraper, full-face respirator or dust mask and goggles, ear defenders, sanding block, dividers, electric soldering iron, small penknife

OTHER USEFUL TOOLS
selection of knives

Kitchen workboards

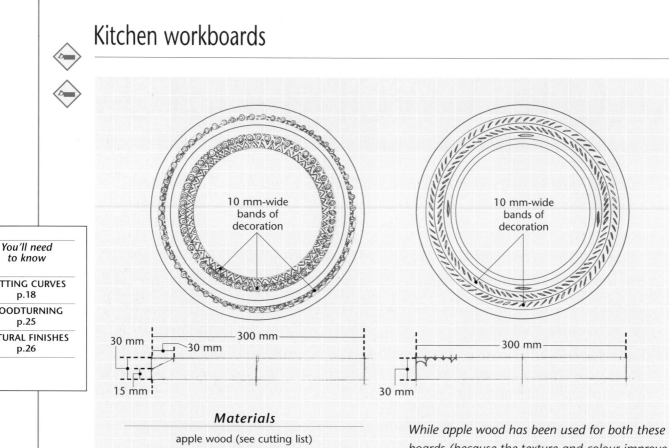

10 mm-wide
bands of
decoration

10 mm-wide
bands of
decoration

30 mm · 30 mm · 300 mm

15 mm

300 mm

30 mm

Materials

apple wood (see cutting list)
countersunk steel screws to fit lathe face plate
sandpaper grades 100 to 300
olive oil and lint-free cotton cloth to apply it

Cutting List

2 pieces apple wood 300 x 300 x 30 mm (boards)

While apple wood has been used for both these boards (because the texture and colour improve with age), you could replace it with just about any fruit wood instead, such as pear, cherry or plum. Avoid exotic woods that leach sap or woods that smell when they are wet.

PYROGRAPHY BOARD

1 Check the slab of wood to make sure that it is absolutely sound throughout, with no knots or splits. Make a point of having a really close look at the end grain, because there is nothing quite so disappointing as going to all the trouble of turning and decorating, only to see the board split in half. Look at the two faces of the board to see which is best. Set your compasses to the largest radius that can be accommodated on the board, and draw a circle on the poorer face (see Fig 1). Mark the centre point with a cross, making sure that it is clearly visible.

FIG 1

FIG 2

TIP

Woodturning is potentially dangerous. Always read the lathe manufacturer's instructions before switching on the power, and work through the following safety checklist.
Always wear a full-face respirator or dust mask and goggles. Remove jewellery and tie back your hair. Never work at a lathe if you are taking medication. Always let someone know before you go off to work on the lathe. Make sure that you are near a phone. If children want to watch, make them wear dust masks, goggles and ear defenders, and keep them well away from the lathe.

2 Prepare the circle for the carved board at the same time as the pyrography board. Fit the scroll saw with a large-toothed blade and adjust the tension so that the blade "pings" when plucked. Fret out the two discs (see Fig 2). These are the blanks for the boards.

FIG 3

FIG 4

3 Set the lathe face plate flat on one of the blanks and align it so that the drawn cross is accurately centred. Clamp the blank to the bench with the holdfast and fix the face plate to the wood with three or more screws (see Fig 3). Mount the face plate securely on the lathe.

4 Adjust the tool rest so that it is just below the centre of spin. Put on your dust mask, goggles and ear defenders. Switch on the power and use the gouge to turn the wood to a smooth disc. Use the skew chisel to turn a slope around the edge (see Fig 4).

FIG 5

FIG 6

5 When you have achieved a crisp disc, take a fold of medium-grade sandpaper and rub the surface to a smooth finish. Set the dividers to 10 mm and use them to scribe a series of step-offs around the border (see Fig 5). Scribe as many step-offs as you want to decorate.

6 Remove the board from the face plate. Switch on the soldering iron and wait until it is red-hot. Have a practice run on some scrap wood to create a design that you like. Burn the design into the board (see Fig 6). Finally, give it a rub-down with olive oil.

CARVED BOARD

FIG 1

FIG 2

7 Mount the sawn blank on the lathe as described in step 3 for the pyrography board. Turn it to a smooth disc, and then with the skew chisel, round over the edge of the disc so that it is nicely convex in cross-section (see Fig 1). Use sandpaper to tidy up the edge and rub the central plateau to a good finish.

8 Continue shaping the edge of the disc until you have a border about 50 mm wide. Set the dividers to 10 mm and run three step-offs around the centre of the border. Take the round-nosed scraper and sculpt a gully on the innermost edge of the border (see Fig 2). Remove the disc from the lathe and sand the back.

FIG 3

9 Put the disc on the bench. With the small penknife, work around the outer border cutting a series of stop-cuts – cuts that run to a depth of about 3 mm. Run a second series of cuts alongside the first to remove boat-shaped chips of wood and create little pockets (see Fig 3).

FIG 4

10 Repeat the chip-cutting procedure as described, only this time work in the opposite direction so that the chips form a chevron, like a stylized ear of wheat (see Fig 4). Brush away the dust and debris, check that the back is smooth, give the wood a wipe over with olive oil, and the board is ready to use.

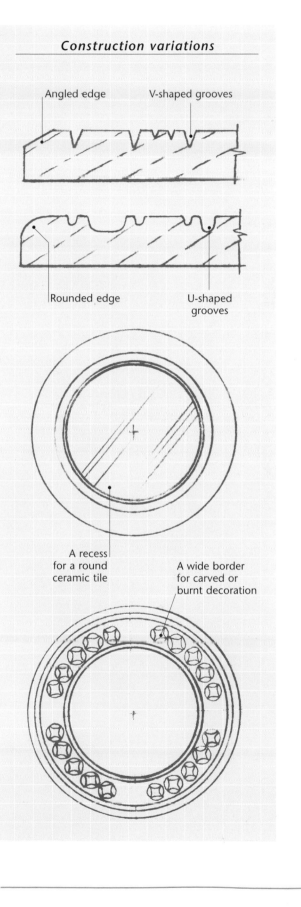

Construction variations

Angled edge   V-shaped grooves

Rounded edge   U-shaped grooves

A recess for a round ceramic tile

A wide border for carved or burnt decoration

TV and video table

The idea for this project came to me when I was watching television and suddenly realized that the whole television set-up looked a mess. Not only was the video recorder sitting on the floor, with the videotapes piled high on a side chair, but worse still, cables and wires snaked all over the place. I decided it would be much neater to have one table housing all the equipment and hiding the wires, which fitted snugly in the corner.

Apart from a couple of dowels, the table is made from birch plywood throughout, and has four swivel wheels on the underside. Its triangular shape allows it to fit into the corner of a room. The idea is that the television sits on the top surface, the video recorder slides on one shelf, videotapes and magazines are stored on the other, and the cables run out of the back corner of the table directly to the sockets. With the surfaces left natural and wiped over with oil, the table is functional, modern and attractive.

If you like the overall idea of the project, but would prefer to have four shelves, or you want to include a rack for videotapes, the design is flexible enough to allow for modifications and you can adapt it to suit your needs.

Essential Tools

workbench with vice and holdfast, pencil, rule, compasses, square, block plane, sanding block, jigsaw, electric drill, 12 mm forstner bit, 7 mm counter-bore bit with a plug cutter to match, screwdriver, awl, paintbrush

OTHER USEFUL TOOLS
cordless screwdriver, power sander, marking knife

TV and video table

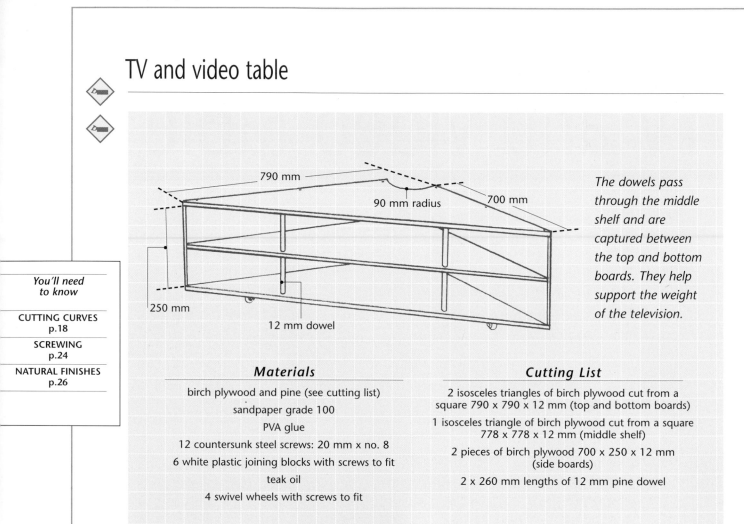

790 mm

90 mm radius

700 mm

250 mm

12 mm dowel

The dowels pass through the middle shelf and are captured between the top and bottom boards. They help support the weight of the television.

Materials

birch plywood and pine (see cutting list)

sandpaper grade 100

PVA glue

12 countersunk steel screws: 20 mm x no. 8

6 white plastic joining blocks with screws to fit

teak oil

4 swivel wheels with screws to fit

Cutting List

2 isosceles triangles of birch plywood cut from a square 790 x 790 x 12 mm (top and bottom boards)

1 isosceles triangle of birch plywood cut from a square 778 x 778 x 12 mm (middle shelf)

2 pieces of birch plywood 700 x 250 x 12 mm (side boards)

2 x 260 mm lengths of 12 mm pine dowel

FIG 1

on what will be the side edges (this indicates where the edge of the side board underneath is). Set the compasses to 90 mm, spike on the right-angled corner of the triangle and strike off a quarter-circle (see Fig 1). Do this on all three boards.

FIG 2

1 Take the top and bottom boards, and the middle shelf, and clean up the edges with the block plane and sandpaper. Make sure that the top and bottom boards are absolutely identical in size. With the pencil, rule a 12 mm border on the face of the top and bottom boards,

2 Use the holdfast to secure the workpiece to the bench – so that the right-angled corner is well clear – and then take the jigsaw and fret out the corner detail (see Fig 2). Repeat this procedure on all three boards.

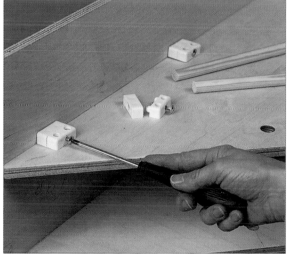

FIG 3

3 Drill the dowel holes with the 12 mm bit. The holes go right through the middle shelf and only half-way through the inside face of the top and bottom boards. Drill holes for the screws with the 7 mm counter-bore bit. Glue and screw the top board to the side boards. Cut plugs and glue them over the screwheads. Fix the middle shelf with the plastic joining blocks (see Fig 3).

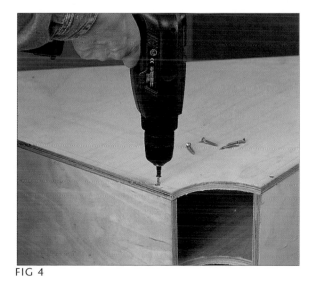

FIG 4

4 Slide the two 12 mm dowels into place, and drill, glue and screw the bottom board into position (see Fig 4). Plug the screws as for the top board. Rub down everything with the graded sandpapers and apply some teak oil.

FIG 5

5 Turn the table over so that the underside of the bottom board is uppermost and draw in the position of the four swivel wheels. Make holes with the awl and screw the wheels in place (see Fig 5). Finally, give the top surface another rub-down with the finest grade of sandpaper, followed by another coat of teak oil. Oil the whole table several more times over the next 48 hours.

TIP

If you like the idea of the project but want to cut costs and go for a more basic structure, you could use faced particleboard instead of plywood, and miss out the glue and screws and use the plastic fixing blocks throughout.

Studio table

Designed to complement the Adjustable Porch Chair on pages 130–135, this table is an absolute classic – a truly beautiful piece of quality modern furniture, a piece that draws its inspiration from medieval trestle tables.

Made from American oak throughout, this table looks equally at home in the studio or dining room. The secret of its appeal is the choice of wood, the generous width and thickness of the boards, and the simplicity of the design. The great thing about the table is that it can be made without cutting any joints: the boards are simply butted or sandwiched and then fitted with hex-head bolts that run through the thickness of the wood. The two X-frames that make up the legs are linked by the tabletop and the under-stretchers in such a way that the whole structure becomes stable. To finish the surface, the wood is wire-brushed to give it a weathered texture and then wiped with Danish oil. If you like this design but are put off by the price of American oak, the alternative is not to reduce costs by buying thinner boards, but to opt for pine instead and slightly increase the thickness of the boards you purchase.

———————————— Essential Tools ————————————

workbench with vice, compasses, pencil, rule, square, bevel gauge, clamps, bench drill press, 10 mm forstner bit, 5 mm twist bit, crosscut saw, block plane, wire brush, sanding block, paintbrush, pilot-countersink bit, electric drill, a screwdriver bit, hacksaw, metal file, allen key to fit the hex-heads, screwdriver

OTHER USEFUL TOOLS
power sander

Studio table

You'll need to know

DRILLING HOLES
p.19

SPECIAL FINISHES
p.27

SCREWING
p.24

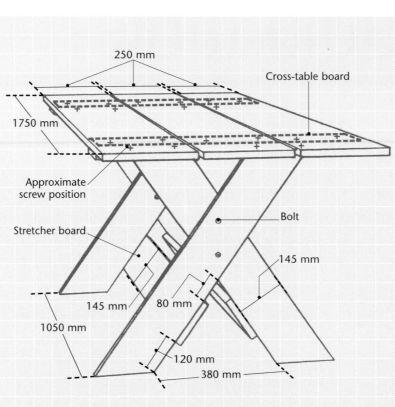

250 mm

Cross-table board

1750 mm

Approximate screw position

Bolt

Stretcher board

145 mm

145 mm   80 mm

1050 mm

120 mm

380 mm

The dimensions of this table and the position of the legs make it suitable for seating six people – one at each end and two on each side.

Materials

American oak (see cutting list)

sandpaper grades 100 to 300

Danish oil

20 countersunk steel screws:
35 mm x no. 8

4 bolts: steel and brass hex-head fasteners complete with threaded steel rod to fit

8 countersunk steel screws:
75 mm x no. 8

Cutting List

all pieces cut from American oak

4 pieces 920 x 145 x 22 mm
(leg boards)

3 pieces 1750 x 250 x 22 mm
(tabletop boards)

2 pieces 755 x 145 x 22 mm
(cross-table boards)

2 pieces 1050 x 145 x 22 mm
(stretcher boards)

2 pieces 145 x 25 x 22 mm
(distance blocks)

FIG 1

FIG 2

1 Take the four 920 mm leg boards, measure 100 mm along from each end, and use the bevel gauge to run a line across from the 100 mm mark to the corner (see Fig 1).

2 Set the leg boards together to form the X-frames and clamp. Mark in the various screw and bolt holes. Drill the holes – 5 mm for the screws and 10 mm for the bolts (see Fig 2).

FIG 3

FIG 5

3 Use the crosscut saw to cut the leg boards to shape. Plane the end grain to a good finish. Use the wire brush to scour out the soft part of the grain, so that the surface feels furrowed to the touch (see Fig 3). Sand lightly. Give all the boards a couple of coats of Danish oil.

5 Cut the threaded rod to length with the hacksaw (to suit the brass hex-heads) and file the ends so that they run smoothly into the hex-heads. Slide the rods through the X-frame leg boards, thread on the hex-heads, and clench them with the allen key (see Fig 5).

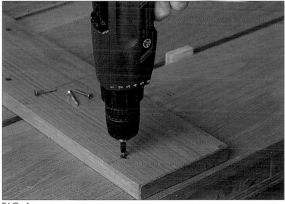

FIG 4

FIG 6

4 Set the three 250 mm-wide tabletop boards face down on the workbench with 15 mm-thick spacers of scrap wood to keep them apart. Place the two cross-table boards in position, and check with the square to make sure the angle between the legs and the table surface is 90°. Drill holes with the pilot-countersink bit and screw them in place using the screwdriver attachment on the drill. Use two 35 mm screws for each crossover of the two boards (see Fig 4). The two cross-table boards should be 1072 mm apart.

6 Butt the X-frame leg boards against the cross-table board, fit and clamp one of the distance blocks and fix with 75 mm screws (see Fig 6). Do this at both ends of the table. Finally, set the stretcher boards in place, on what will be the underside of the X-frame legs, and screw them in position with 35 mm screws.

Turned table lamp

The design of this lamp evolved after considering the technical problems of making a turned lamp with a flex hole down its centre, without using a single piece of expensive wood. The lamp can be used in any room if you fit an appropriate shade. The shape of the form can also be modified to suit your tastes, and the size and power of your lathe.

The lamp base is made from pine throughout. Four small square sections are each planed along one arris (sharp edge) and then glued together in such a way that the four cut-away corners form the flex hole. While the form is still on the lathe, it is stained with a felt-tip pen and burnished with wax. This is a nice, straightforward project if you are new to woodturning – it's inexpensive and there is no need to drill a deep hole for the lamp flex. Although I used a pen for staining the wood, you could also use a spirit-based wood dye, or even a water-based wood dye followed by a coat of varnish. This lamp is made from four sections, however if anyone offers you a single chunk of seasoned pine, don't turn it down.

——— Essential Tools ———

workbench with vice, compasses, pencil, rule, smoothing plane, 4 short sash clamps, bench drill press, 50 mm forstner bit, good-size lathe with an expanding chuck and the capacity to turn a blank bigger than 250 mm in diameter, set of turning tools to include a large gouge, a skew chisel and a round-nosed scraper, full-face respirator or dust mask and goggles, ear defenders, screwdriver

OTHER USEFUL TOOLS
cordless screwdriver, power sander

Turned table lamp

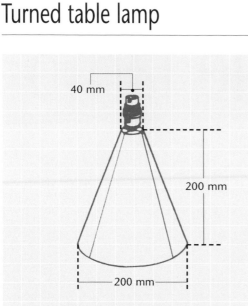

40 mm

200 mm

200 mm

Make sure that the four pine sections you buy are properly seasoned, otherwise the turned form will shrink and split.

Materials

pine (see cutting list)

PVA glue

sandpaper grades 100 to 150

a couple of spirit-based black felt-tip markers

beeswax polish

lint-free cotton cloth to apply the beeswax

lamp head complete with flex,
plug and screws to fit

lampshade to suit

Cutting List

4 pieces pine 200 x 100 x 100 mm

*You'll need
to know*

HAND PLANING
p.20

WOODTURNING
p.25

NATURAL FINISHES
p.26

TIP

Woodturning is potentially dangerous, so be very aware of safety. Always make sure you are suitably dressed, with no dangling hair or jewellery, and no flapping cuffs. Always wear a dust mask and goggles, or a full-face respirator mask; ear defenders are also recommended. Keep children away.

FIG 1

1 Take the four 200 mm-long pine sections and group them four-square so that the best faces are outermost. Plane back the central corners 10 mm (see Fig 1).

FIG 2

2 Regroup the blocks, clamping them together in a trial run to ensure that the mating faces come together tight and true. If necessary, use the plane to cut back the faces. Take the stack apart. Then smear PVA glue on the mating faces of two neighbouring blocks and clamp up (see Fig 2). Repeat this procedure with the other two blocks. When the glue is dry, glue and clamp the paired blocks to make the single four-block blank with a small central hole.

FIG 3

3 Tap a stick of scrap in each end of the central hole. Use the 50 mm forstner bit to bore to a depth of about 10 mm in one end of the block. Mount the blank on the expanding chuck and draw up the tailstock centre (see Fig 3). Turn the wood over by hand to test all is correct.

FIG 4

4 Arrange the tool rest so that it is clear of the workpiece. Put on the protective gear and tie back your hair. Use the large gouge to turn the square section into the largest possible cylinder (see Fig 4). Use the skew chisel to skim the wood to a smooth finish. Tighten up the tailstock centre.

FIG 5

5 Use the gouge to turn the cylinder into a rough cone shape (the base of the cone is nearest to the expanding chuck). Change over to the round-nosed scraper and skew chisel and continue turning until the lines of the cone are clean and smooth (see Fig 5).

FIG 6

6 Take the felt-tip pen and run it up and down the spinning cone until the surface is completely black (see Fig 6). Do this several times to ensure even coverage. Use the sandpaper and beeswax to burnish the surface to a high-shine finish. Screw-fit the lamp head to the top of the cone, join up the flex and attach the shade.

Bathroom cabinet

The design for this project, like many designs, grew and evolved. When we are planning projects, we often sit around with pencil, paper and a cup of tea, and figure out the options. In this instance, I started out with an idea for no more than a rail for a roller towel. Then Gill suggested that we have a rail with a shelf. I thought that we might as well have a couple of shelves. Gill volunteered that perhaps we ought to add two doors, with attractive hinges and tiny knobs – so it went on. Before long we finished up with a project for a little cupboard complete with a rail, two doors, a carved turnbuckle, two whittled knobs, and routed details.

The cabinet is mainly made from laminated pine. The two shelves are housed in the end boards, while the three vertical posts are dowelled into the shelves, and the rail is captured between the end boards. To finish the cabinet, it is rubbed down with graded sandpapers and wiped with teak oil.

Essential Tools

workbench with vice and holdfast, compass, pencil, rule, square, tracing paper, scroll saw, router and router table, 4 mm and 13 mm groove cutters, cove cutter, 2 long sash clamps, bench drill press, 15 mm forstner bit, electric drill, 6 mm twist bit, 6 mm dowel marker studs, mallet, penknife, screwdriver, sanding block, paintbrush

OTHER USEFUL TOOLS
cordless screwdriver, power sander, dividers, marking knife

Bathroom cabinet

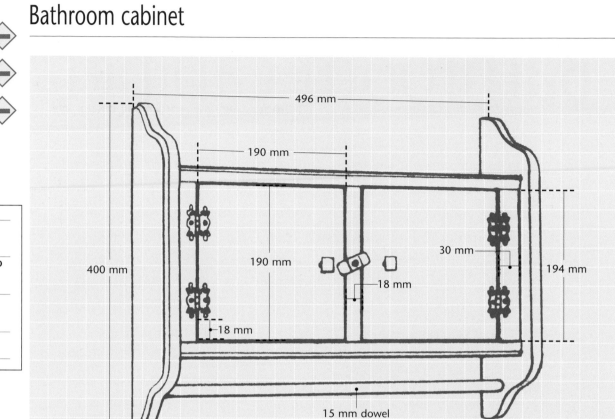

496 mm
190 mm
400 mm
190 mm
30 mm
194 mm
18 mm
18 mm
15 mm dowel

Materials

pine and plywood (see cutting list)

guide strip of waste wood: 350 mm long

12 x 30 mm fixing dowels, 6 mm in diameter

PVA glue

1 brass dome-headed screw: 30 mm x no. 8

sandpaper grades 100 to 150

4 decorative brass hinges with brass screws to
fit: size and design to suit

teak oil

Cutting List

2 pieces pine 400 x 150 x 18 mm (end boards)

2 pieces pine 476 x 126 x 18 mm (shelf boards)

1 piece plywood 476 x 210 x 4 mm (back board)

3 pieces pine 194 x 30 x 18 mm (vertical battens)

476 mm length of 15 mm pine dowel (rail)

2 pieces pine 190 x 190 x 18 mm (doors)

The length of the vertical battens allows for slightly loose-fitting doors, to avoid problems if the wood gets damp and expands. The template below is for half of an end board.

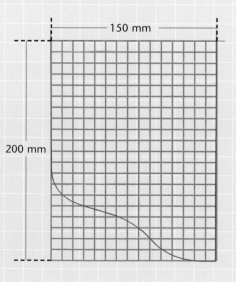

150 mm

200 mm

FIG 1

1 Take the 150 mm-wide end boards and use the pencil, square, rule and tracing paper to carefully set out all the lines that go to make up the design (see Fig 1). Although we have specified 150 mm-wide boards at 400 mm long, if you can get the design out of boards left over from another project, that is fine. In this project we have actually used a wider piece of wood flawed by a couple of badly placed knots.

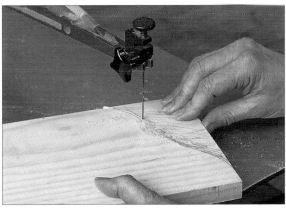

FIG 2

2 Label the best faces of the two end boards and then fret out the marked design on the scroll saw (see Fig 2). Work slowly, feeding the wood forward so that the blade is presented with the line of next cut. If you feel the blade pulling or the workpiece going off course, ease back and realign the cut. If the going gets heavy, switch off the power and check the blade. Maybe the blade needs changing or re-tensioning, or alternatively, perhaps the wood is damp.

FIG 3

3 Fit the 13 mm groove cutter in the router and attach the router to its table. Set one of the end boards flat on the bench, with the inside face uppermost, and clamp it into position. Clamp the guide strip across the board so that the router is able to run alongside it, with the cutter centred on the marked-out housing groove. Plunge the router forward and cut the groove. Make several passes to end up with a depth of 18 mm. Re-run this procedure for all four housings. With the bench drill press and the 15 mm bit, drill the rail holes to a depth of about 8 mm.

When you are ready to cut the cove detail on the shelf ends and edges, fit the cove cutter in the router, and move the fence back out of the way. Switch on the power, wait until the bit is running at full speed, and follow the bearing guide to make the cut (see Fig 3). If you are new to the procedure, have a trial run on some scrap wood.

Towel rail

The brief for this project was to make a contemporary towel rail containing traditional elements, but which was not a copy of a historical original. It had to look modern, and yet, in spirit at least, it had to be a cottage piece. The design needed to be suitable for a beginner with the minimum of tools. As you can see, while this towel rail has many of the elements that you would expect to see on a classic cottage piece – pierced ends, rounded tops, handle holes, arched foot and an ornate bottom rail – these are no more than stylized interpretations, achieved with the minimum of tools.

    The whole thing is made from pine, with the end boards fretted out on the scroll saw, and the bottom rail fretted and then shaped with the spokeshave. All four rails are wedge-tenoned into the end boards. The wood is left in its natural state. It is a very easy item to make – the perfect project for a long weekend. If you like the notion of making a cottage design and yet do not feel up to turning complex rails on a lathe, this project is for you.

Essential Tools

workbench with vice and holdfast, compasses, pencil, rule, square, bench drill press, 12 mm and 55 mm forstner bits, scroll saw, 2 long sash clamps, 12 mm and 20 mm bevel-edge chisels, router and router table, 10 mm groove cutter, spokeshave, sanding block, penknife

OTHER USEFUL TOOLS
cordless screwdriver, power sander, electric drill, dividers, marking knife

Towel rail

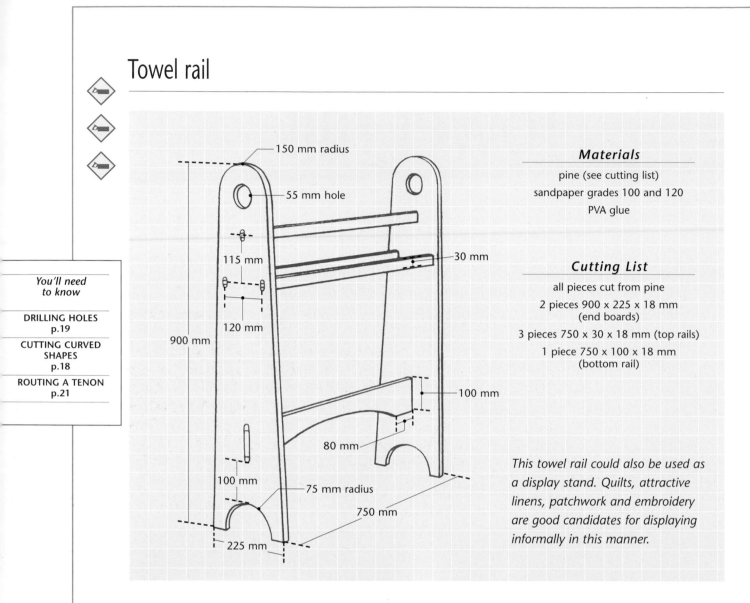

150 mm radius
55 mm hole
115 mm
30 mm
120 mm
900 mm
100 mm
80 mm
100 mm
75 mm radius
750 mm
225 mm

Materials

pine (see cutting list)
sandpaper grades 100 and 120
PVA glue

Cutting List

all pieces cut from pine
2 pieces 900 x 225 x 18 mm
(end boards)
3 pieces 750 x 30 x 18 mm (top rails)
1 piece 750 x 100 x 18 mm
(bottom rail)

This towel rail could also be used as a display stand. Quilts, attractive linens, patchwork and embroidery are good candidates for displaying informally in this manner.

FIG 1

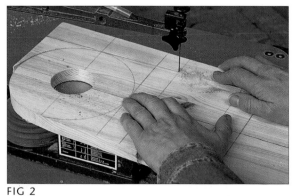

FIG 2

1 Draw in centre-lines on the end boards. Set the compasses to a radius of 75 mm and draw out the top and bottom details. Use the rule to link up the details (see Fig 1).

2 Bore the handle hole with the 55 mm forstner bit and fret out the form on the scroll saw. Cut in from both ends of the wood to meet at the middle (see Fig 2).

FIG 3

FIG 5

3 Drill the ends of the mortise holes with the 12 mm forstner bit. Clamp the workpiece flat on the bench and chop out the remaining waste with the 12 mm bevel-edge chisel (see Fig 3). Work from both sides so that the wood is not damaged when the chisel exits.

5 Cut out the shape of the bottom rail on the scroll saw and then use the spokeshave to bring the sawn edge to a rounded, smoothly curved finish (see Fig 5). Use the spokeshave to chamfer the edges of the three top rails. Sand all the edges and faces to a smooth finish.

FIG 4

FIG 6

4 Fit the 10 mm groove cutter in the router and attach the router to its table. Draw the fence back, and set the bit to a height of 3 mm. Pass the rails through the router and cut shoulders on both side faces. Reduce the bit height to 1.5 mm and cut shoulders on the top and bottom edge faces (see Fig 4).

6 With the penknife and chisels, carefully shape the square ends of the rails to fit the round-ended mortises (see Fig 6). When you have achieved a push-fit, run two saw kerfs (cuts) into the ends of the tenons. Finally, glue and wedge the rails in place, and sand the towel rail to a smooth finish, especially the top of the rails.

Sauna bench

This stylish seat is suitable for a bathroom or sauna, because it resists steam and hot water. Glue has not been used in its construction. It has been designed so that it can be built in the space of a day with the minimum of tools and expertise – there are no joints to make and there is no need for expensive tools. Material costs are low – we have opted for pine instead of using expensive endangered species such as mahogany, and the bench is put together without pricey brass or stainless-steel fittings.

After drawing lots of sketches and playing around with bits of card and scrap wood, we came up with this novel design. It's wonderfully simple – all the components are made from pine section, and the bench is held together with four threaded rods complete with nuts, washers and screws. We kept costs down by using zinc-plated rod, however you could improve on the quality of the finish by using stainless steel. Note how the inclusion of two stretcher pieces set into the top of the seat acts as an anti-wracking device (stops it twisting) and keeps the structure square.

Essential Tools

workbench with vice and holdfast, pencil, rule, square, bench drill press, 6 mm twist bit, block plane, sanding block, clamps, screwdriver, pair of wrenches to fit the nuts, hacksaw, file

OTHER USEFUL TOOLS
cordless screwdriver, power sander

Sauna bench

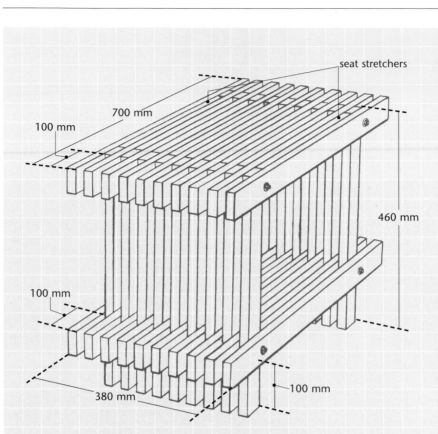

seat stretchers

700 mm

100 mm

100 mm

380 mm

460 mm

100 mm

You'll need
to know

DRILLING HOLES
p.19

HAND PLANING
p.20

SCREWING
p.24

Materials

pine (see cutting list)

sandpaper grades 100
and 120

4 countersunk steel screws:
30 mm x no. 8

4 x 400 mm lengths of
plated 6 mm threaded rod
with 8 nuts and 8 washers
to fit

Cutting List

all pieces cut from pine

20 pieces 700 x 50 x 20 mm
(seat and undershelf)

18 pieces 460 x 50 x 20 mm
(legs)

2 pieces 400 x 50 x 20 mm
(seat stretchers)

*The dimensions given are for a single-seat bench, but you could
double the length of the seat and undershelf pieces so that the
bench is long enough to stretch out on.*

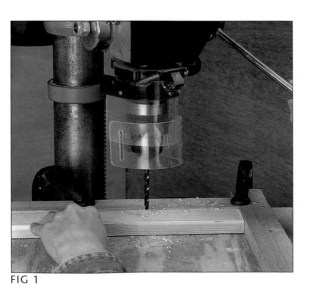

FIG 1

TIP

**The jig ensures that holes can be
drilled accurately. Run the drill in and
out repeatedly, in order to clear the
waste from the hole, and to allow the
bit to cool down. Brush the debris off
the jig after each boring.**

1 Mark the position of the holes for the
threaded rod – see the working drawing –
and build a jig from scrap wood. Clamp the
jig to the table of the bench drill press and use the
6 mm bit to bore the holes (see Fig 1).

FIG 2

2 Use the block plane and the medium-grade sandpaper to remove the sharp edges from all 40 component parts (see Fig 2).

FIG 3

3 Clamp and screw the first seat stretcher in place and start sliding the components on to the threaded rods (see Fig 3). Be careful not to damage the thread or split the wood.

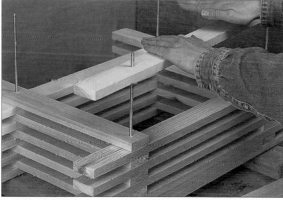

FIG 4

4 Ease each piece down the threaded rods, making sure the best edges form the upper surface of the seat (see Fig 4).

FIG 5

5 When you have screwed the other stretcher in place, and fitted the last two seat and undershelf pieces, use the square to ensure that the whole structure is true. Finally, clench the nuts with the wrenches (see Fig 5), saw the ends off the threaded rods with the hacksaw and file them to a smooth finish.

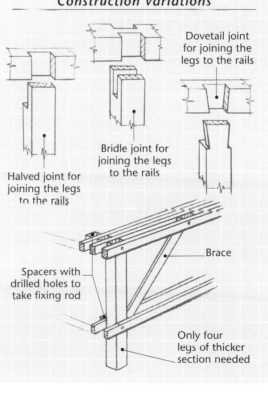

Construction variations

Dovetail joint for joining the legs to the rails

Bridle joint for joining the legs to the rails

Halved joint for joining the legs to the rails

Brace

Spacers with drilled holes to take fixing rod

Only four legs of thicker section needed

Garden trug

This pretty garden trug or basket is reminiscent of the beautiful split wood baskets that were popular in Edwardian times. Prints of the period depicting garden scenes often show the lady of the house gliding around the garden with a parasol in one hand and a trug in the other. A trug is perfectly suited to carrying small tools and garden produce. You might use it when weeding a border, or when cutting flowers. Trugs are also suitable for indoor use – their design makes them ideal as a feature in the kitchen, perhaps for holding cutlery or bread, or even for decorative use as a table centrepiece.

The trug is made from pine throughout. The two side boards are worked on the scroll saw, the slats are pinned in place, the fretted uprights are screwed to the side boards, and the handle is simply captured between the supports. A unique feature of this design is the whittled stretcher handle, which has a curvaceous form and dappled texture. To finish, it was colourwashed with acrylic paint, followed by a couple of coats of teak oil.

— Essential Tools —

workbench with vice and holdfast, pencil, rule, compasses, square, bevel gauge, clamp, jigsaw, bench drill press, 15 mm forstner bit, scroll saw, pin hammer, screwdriver, knife, block plane, sanding block, 2 paintbrushes

OTHER USEFUL TOOLS
cordless screwdriver, power sander, electric drill, marking knife, bandsaw

Garden trug

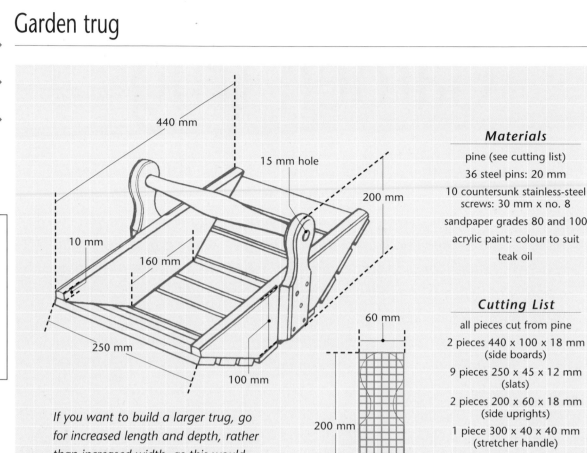

440 mm

15 mm hole

200 mm

10 mm

160 mm

250 mm

60 mm

100 mm

200 mm

If you want to build a larger trug, go for increased length and depth, rather than increased width, as this would make it rather ungainly. The template for the side upright is shown right.

Materials

pine (see cutting list)

36 steel pins: 20 mm

10 countersunk stainless-steel
screws: 30 mm x no. 8

sandpaper grades 80 and 100

acrylic paint: colour to suit

teak oil

Cutting List

all pieces cut from pine

2 pieces 440 x 100 x 18 mm
(side boards)

9 pieces 250 x 45 x 12 mm
(slats)

2 pieces 200 x 60 x 18 mm
(side uprights)

1 piece 300 x 40 x 40 mm
(stretcher handle)

You'll need to know

CUTTING CURVED
SHAPES
p.18

NAILING AND
PINNING
p.24

WHITTLING
p.25

FIG 1

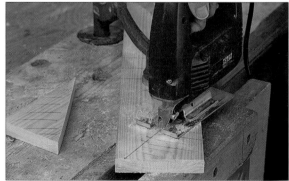

FIG 2

1 Take the two prepared boards at 440 mm long and 100 mm wide, and use the bevel gauge, rule and square to carefully draw out the profile of the sides, complete with the centre-line and the position of the slats (see Fig 1).

2 Clamp the workpiece firmly on the bench so that the waste is hanging clear, and use the jigsaw to cut out the profile to the waste side of the drawn line (see Fig 2). Always cut from the base edge through to the top corner.

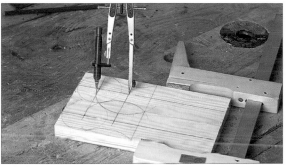

FIG 3

3 Clamp the two 60 mm-wide side uprights together. Use the square, rule and compasses to set out the round-topped shape (see working drawing) complete with a centre-line and the position of the handle hole (see Fig 3).

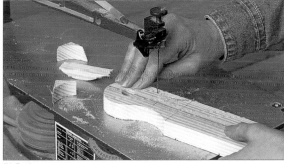

FIG 4

4 Drill the handle holes with the 15 mm forstner bit. Use the scroll saw to fret out the design, with the line of cut set slightly to the waste side of the drawn line (see Fig 4).

FIG 5

5 With the two side boards bottom edge uppermost and parallel to each other, bridge them with the slats. Check the alignment with the square, and then nail the slats in position with two pins at each end (see Fig 5).

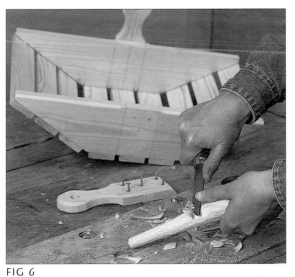

FIG 6

TIP

When you are whittling, control the knife by working with the wood braced tightly against your thumb, and making a "pushing" cut. Keep both the knife and the workpiece moving so you achieve a uniform section. Use a selection of knives of different weights and sizes, to achieve a variety of cuts.

---

6 Screw one side upright in place. To make the stretcher handle, whittle the 40 mm section to a cylinder with the knife, working from centre to end. Continue until the ends fit the 15 mm holes and the form is nicely curved (see Fig 6). Capture the handle between the two side uprights and fix with screws. Finally, tidy up all the end-grain surfaces with the block plane and rub down the trug with sandpaper. Dilute the paint in water to make a wash and brush on. When it is dry, lay on two coats of teak oil.

Doll's house

Most children really enjoy playing with doll's houses, but many parents find them something of a nuisance. The problem is that they are usually bulky, fragile, and difficult to store. So we have designed a doll's house that can be flat-packed. When the children have finished playing with it, you simply pull it apart and slide it under the bed. The design is so simple that you can even let the children put it together themselves, like a construction kit. We have stylized the design so that children can let their imaginations run riot: it can be a townhouse, or a cottage, or perhaps a garage for cars, or even a school. There are many exciting possibilities.

The house is made of 6 mm birch plywood, and the various forms are slotted and shaped so that the parts slide together easily. The scroll saw makes it simple to construct. Most of the corners are rounded, and the whole thing is finished with child-friendly acrylic paint. Check with the manufacturer to ensure that a paint really is suitable for applying to a children's toy – it must have no harmful effects if the toy is put in the mouth.

——— Essential Tools ———

workbench with vice and holdfast, compasses, pencil, rule, square, bevel gauge, scroll saw, electric drill, 5 mm and 8 mm twist bits, sanding block, 2 paintbrushes

OTHER USEFUL TOOLS
power sander

Doll's house

You'll need to know

CUTTING CURVED
SHAPES
p.18

SANDING
p.26

PAINTED FINISHES
p.27

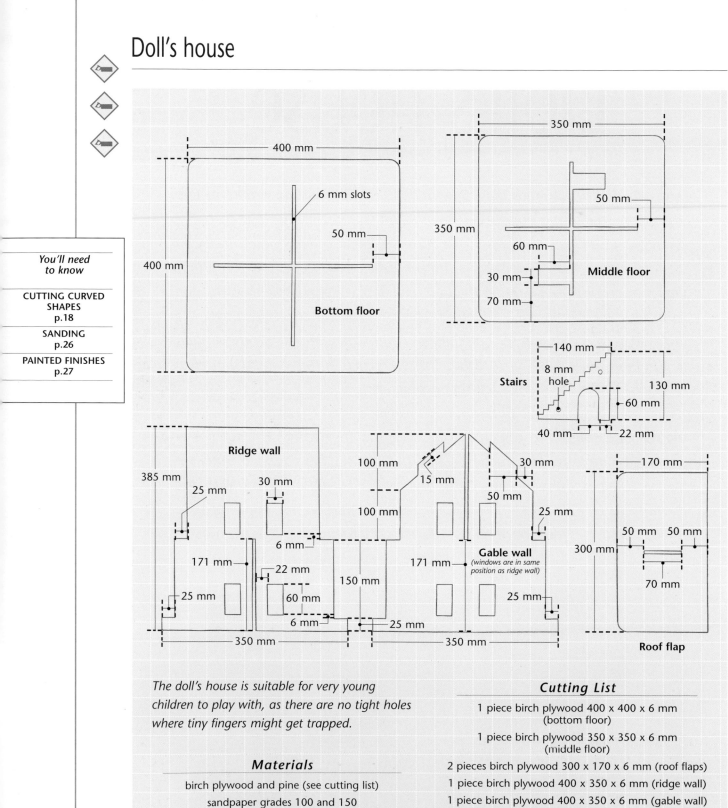

Bottom floor — 400 mm × 400 mm, 6 mm slots, 50 mm

Middle floor — 350 mm × 350 mm, 50 mm, 60 mm, 30 mm, 70 mm

Stairs — 140 mm, 8 mm hole, 130 mm, 60 mm, 40 mm, 22 mm

Ridge wall — 385 mm, 25 mm, 30 mm, 6 mm, 171 mm, 22 mm, 25 mm, 60 mm, 6 mm, 350 mm

Gable wall (windows are in same position as ridge wall) — 100 mm, 15 mm, 100 mm, 30 mm, 50 mm, 171 mm, 150 mm, 25 mm, 25 mm, 350 mm

Roof flap — 170 mm, 300 mm, 50 mm, 50 mm, 70 mm

The doll's house is suitable for very young children to play with, as there are no tight holes where tiny fingers might get trapped.

Materials

birch plywood and pine (see cutting list)
sandpaper grades 100 and 150
acrylic paint: red, yellow, pink, blue and green
matt acrylic varnish

Cutting List

1 piece birch plywood 400 x 400 x 6 mm (bottom floor)

1 piece birch plywood 350 x 350 x 6 mm (middle floor)

2 pieces birch plywood 300 x 170 x 6 mm (roof flaps)

1 piece birch plywood 400 x 350 x 6 mm (ridge wall)

1 piece birch plywood 400 x 350 x 6 mm (gable wall)

4 pieces birch plywood 140 x 130 x 6 mm (stairs)

2 x 40 mm lengths of 8 mm pine dowel

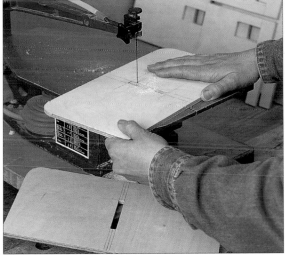

FIG 1

FIG 2

FIG 3

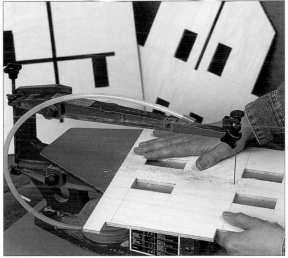

FIG 4

1 Study the working drawings carefully to see how the whole thing works and slots together, and then use the rule, bevel gauge and square to set out each piece of plywood with all the lines that make up the design (see Fig 1). Shade in the waste areas up to the drawn line.

2 Fit a new fine blade in the scroll saw and tension it until it "pings" when plucked, then start fretting out the various parts (see Fig 2). When you are cutting the slots, make sure that you keep on the waste side of the drawn lines, so the slots are exactly 6 mm wide (or to a maximum of 0.5 mm wider, making 6.5 mm).

3 When you come to an enclosed area – such as the doors or the roof slots – drill pilot holes with the 5 mm bit. Unhitch the scroll saw blade, pass it through the hole, and then refit it and continue as already described (see Fig 3). Be careful not to twist the blade at the turns.

4 Run through a trial fitting of the two walls (see Fig 4). If the slots are too tight, wrap a sheet of fine-grade sandpaper around a piece of waste plywood and sand them to fit. Aim to increase the width of the slots to a maximum of 6.5 mm. Be careful not to rub so hard that you reveal the inner veneers of the plywood.

FIG 5

5 Slide the bottom floor over the walls and check that it fits well – it should sit flat on all four of the lower support steps. Slide the middle floor in place so that it settles on all four of the upper support steps (see Fig 5). Once again, you might need to adjust the slots with fine-grade sandpaper. The best way of sanding is to rest the workpiece flat on the bench, so that the offending edge is as near as possible to the worksurface.

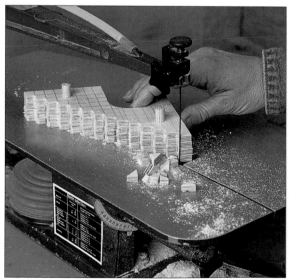

FIG 6

6 Take one of the stair pieces and draw on a 10 mm grid, the outline of the stairs, arched door and dowel holes. Stack the four stair pieces with the gridded piece uppermost, then drill holes with the 8 mm bit and slide in the dowels. With the scroll saw, cut the shapes of the stairs and door through the whole stack (see Fig 6).

FIG 7

7 Take the sanding block and sandpaper and rub all the edges to a good, smooth finish (see Fig 7). Aim for slightly rounded edges. A good way of testing for burrs or sharp edges that you have missed is to feel the forms with your fingertips, keeping your eyes closed.

TIP

Of all the projects in this book, this is the only one where you cannot cut costs – children's toys must be safe. You must use best-quality birch plywood, because it is strong and splinter-proof. It is essential to use paints (and varnishes) that are described by the manufacturer as being safe for children: on no account use household or car paints, because they may contain toxic substances.

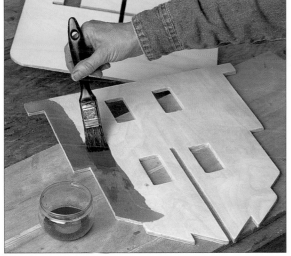

FIG 8

FIG 9

8 Mix the paint with a small amount of water to make a thin wash, apply with a brush (see Fig 8) and let it dry. If you want the colour to be darker, you simply paint on repeat washes until you have the right density of colour. Let the washes dry between coats.

9 When the paint is completely dry – and this might take a couple of days – give the house another rub-down with the graded sandpaper and brush on the varnish. Repeat this procedure a couple of times until the finish feels super-smooth to the touch (see Fig 9).

Construction variations

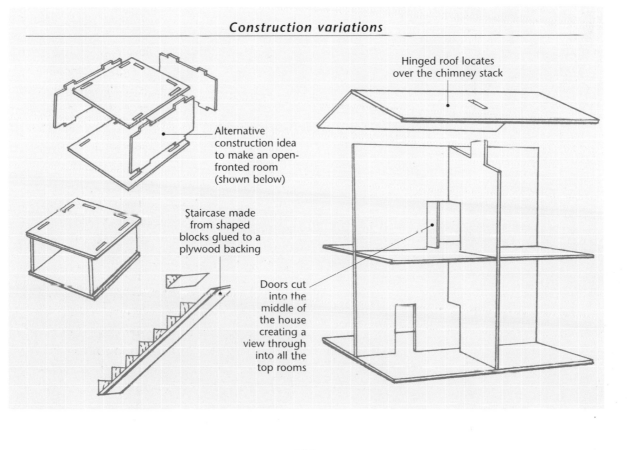

Hinged roof locates over the chimney stack

Alternative construction idea to make an open-fronted room (shown below)

Staircase made from shaped blocks glued to a plywood backing

Doors cut into the middle of the house creating a view through into all the top rooms

Child's folk art chest

When our two sons were about five years old, we made them a traditional six-board chest. It was only a box painted blue, with rope handles and an old map pasted on the underside of the lid, but they thought that it was wonderful. In their imaginations it became a treasure chest and numerous other exciting things. When they were older, it was used to store clothes.

The chest is made from pine throughout. The front and back boards are screwed to the end boards, with the base board captured and screwed between. Rope handles are threaded and knotted through blocks. The lid is simply set flush with the back and hinged. The painted design is in the style of the naive designs on old American folk art chests. Although we have used red, white and blue, and stars and stripes, we have not painted the chest with the specific imagery of the American or British flags. The stripes are painted with the aid of masking tape; the stars are created by cutting a star from a scrap of plywood and using it as a stamp.

Essential Tools

workbench with vice, compasses, pencil, rule, square, scroll saw, electric drill, 6 mm counter-bore bit with a plug cutter to match, screwdriver bit, block plane, clamps, bench drill press, 10 mm and 5 mm twist bits, pilot-countersink bit, sanding block, scissors, 20 mm bevel-edge chisel, artist's paintbrush, screwdriver, paintbrush

OTHER USEFUL TOOLS
power sander

Child's folk art chest

**You'll need
to know**

CUTTING CURVED
SHAPES
p.18

PAINTED FINISHES
p.27

FIXING HINGES
p.25

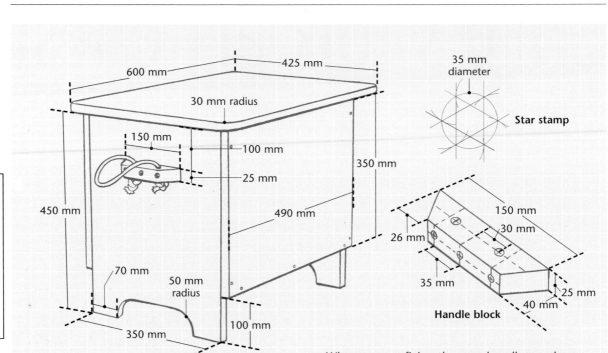

600 mm — 425 mm

30 mm radius

35 mm
diameter

Star stamp

150 mm

100 mm

25 mm

350 mm

450 mm

490 mm

150 mm

30 mm

26 mm

70 mm

50 mm
radius

35 mm

100 mm

25 mm

40 mm

350 mm

Handle block

*When you are fixing the rope handles, make
sure that you make the loops much smaller than
the size of your child's head, or the handles will
present a safety hazard.*

Materials

pine (see cutting list)
30 countersunk steel screws: 30 mm x no. 8
PVA glue
sandpaper grades 100 and 150
6 countersunk steel screws: 35 mm x no. 8
2 x 300 mm lengths of soft hemp rope
masking tape and scissors
acrylic paint: red, white and blue
2 steel hinges: 50 x 18 mm with screws to fit
Danish oil

Cutting List

all pieces cut from pine
2 pieces 490 x 350 x 18 mm (front and back boards)
2 pieces 450 x 350 x 18 mm (end boards)
1 piece 454 x 350 x 18 mm (base board)
1 piece 600 x 425 x 18 mm (lid board)
2 pieces 150 x 40 x 25 mm (handle blocks)

FIG 1

1 Check all the wood to make sure that it is
free from splits. Take the prepared boards
and use the rule, square and compasses to
draw out all the lines that make up the design. Set
out the curve of the lid corners with a 30 mm
radius, and the foot detail on the end boards with
a radius of 50 mm (see Fig 1). Double-check the
measurements and shade in selected areas to
avoid confusion when cutting out. Draw the
shape of the handle blocks, complete with holes.

FIG 2

2 Fret out the various shapes on the scroll saw. When you are cutting the curves, run the line of cut to the waste side of the drawn line (see Fig 2). Have a trial fitting to see how the box comes together. Pay particular attention to the fit of the base board.

FIG 3

3 With the 6 mm counter-bore bit, drill pilot holes through the front and back boards. Using the drill and screwdriver attachment, screw them to the end boards with the 30 mm screws (see Fig 3). The top edges should be flush. Make checks with the square. Cut plugs with the plug cutter and glue them over the screws.

FIG 4

4 Trim the base board to fit between the sides of the chest and fix with 30 mm screws, using the drill and screwdriver attachment, as described in step 3 (see Fig 4). Turn the chest upright to see whether it stands firm. If it rocks, the feet need trimming with the block plane.

FIG 5

5 Cut the handle blocks with the scroll saw and draw in the position of the holes: two 10 mm holes for the ropes, and three 5 mm holes for the screws. Clamp to the bench drill press and bore the holes (see Fig 5). Countersink the screwholes with the pilot-countersink bit and sand the blocks to a smooth finish.

FIG 6

6 Measure 100 mm down from the top of the chest, and centre and screw the handle blocks in place with 35 mm screws (see Fig 6). Take a 300 mm length of rope, thread it through the holes and knot the ends. Do figure-of-eight knots so they cannot slip and come undone.

FIG 7

7 To make the stamp, set the compasses to a radius of 35 mm and draw a circle on scrap wood. With the compasses at the same radius, make step-offs around the circumference of the circle and strike arcs. Use the pencil and rule to draw lines between alternate intersections, so you end up with a six-pointed star (see Fig 7).

FIG 8

8 Position the chest with the front face uppermost. Measure 50 mm in from all four edges and use the pencil and rule to draw a border or frame. Divide up the inside area vertically, so that you have four equal horizontal bands each about 60 mm wide. From top to bottom number the bands 1, 2, 3, and 4. Cover the outer frame and bands 2 and 4 with masking tape. Smooth the tape in place. Brush red acrylic paint over bands 1 and 3, painting well over the edges of the tape. Leave it to dry (see Fig 8).

FIG 9

9 When the red paint is dry, carefully peel off the horizontal strips of tape to reveal beautiful, crisp edges (see Fig 9). Stick masking tape over the bands of red to safeguard them.

FIG 10

10 Paint the bands that you have just revealed with blue paint (see Fig 10). Let the paint dry and carefully peel away all the masking tape on the bands and borders. You should be left with a crisply painted panel. At this point, if you so wish, you could paint similar bands on the lid of the chest.

TIP

If you like the idea of a printed design, but are not keen on the stars, you could cut an alternative shape, or try using other items as stamps, such as corks or leaves. Use paint straight from the tube or bottle, so that it is a thick consistency and will not run.

FIG 11

11 Fret out the star on the scroll saw, sand the edges to a smooth finish, and drive a 30 mm screw into its centre to use like a handle. Spread a generous daub of white paint on a piece of card, then press the star in the paint and start stamping (see Fig 11). Try to do the stamping with a crisp on-and-off action, so the images do not smudge.

FIG 12

12 Finally, when the paint is dry, use the chisel to cut recesses for the hinges and screw them in place. Give all the surfaces a rub-down with fine-grade sandpaper, followed by a coat of Danish oil (see Fig 12).

Kitchen trolley

Now at last you can have the custom-made kitchen trundle trolley of your dreams! A modern classic, this beautifully designed kitchen workstation is made from cool, blonde maple. The woven basket drawer is English willow, the towel bar is stainless steel, the worktop is made from chunky sections, and the trolley is mounted on four super-smooth swivel-turn wheels. This is an amazingly stylish and functional piece – perfect for the modern home.

As for the making process, study our designs first, purchase a ready-made willow basket, the wheels and stainless-steel fittings, and then modify the dimensions and details to suit your needs. It's an easy project to build. The horizontal members – the front and back stretchers, and the back rail – are tenoned into the legs to make two H-frames, and then the two frames are linked by the side rails, the top board and the shelf slats. The wheels are bolted into pilot holes, while the top slab is held in place with screwed blocks and turnbuckles. The wood is finished by repeatedly rubbing down, oiling, waxing and burnishing to a sheen finish with a cotton cloth.

Essential Tools

workbench with vice, pencil, rule, square, biscuit jointer, 4 sash clamps or clamp heads, good selection of G-clamps, jigsaw, block plane, scraper plane, bench drill press, 25 mm forstner bit, 3 mm and 5 mm twist bits and a twist bit to fit the diameter of your wheel bolts, 15 mm bevel-edge chisel, mallet, mitre saw, router and router table, 12 mm groove cutter, knife, tenon saw, smoothing plane, screwdriver, sanding block, pilot-countersink bit, socket and wrench to fit the size of your wheel bolt, paintbrush

OTHER USEFUL TOOLS
cordless screwdriver, power sander, electric drill, dividers, marking knife, bandsaw

Kitchen trolley

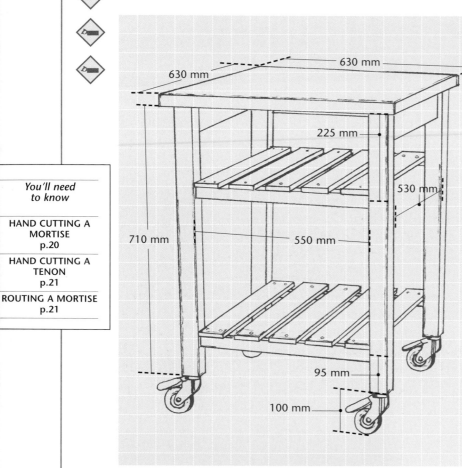

You'll need to know

HAND CUTTING A MORTISE
p.20

HAND CUTTING A TENON
p.21

ROUTING A MORTISE
p.21

630 mm

630 mm

225 mm

530 mm

710 mm   550 mm

95 mm

100 mm

Materials

maple (see cutting list)

pack of jointer biscuits

PVA glue

sandpaper grades 150 to 300

4 swivel-turn wheels (integral foot brakes), to stand about 100 mm from the floor

Danish oil

28 countersunk stainless-steel screws: 30 mm x no. 8

stainless-steel towel rack

Cutting List

all pieces cut from maple

5 pieces 630 x 140 x 30 mm (worktop)

4 pieces 710 x 50 x 50 mm (legs)

2 pieces 530 x 80 x 20 mm (side rails)

1 piece 510 x 80 x 20 mm (back rail)

4 pieces 550 x 30 x 30 mm (stretchers)

10 pieces 590 x 70 x 12 mm (shelf slats)

If your wheels are a different size to those specified, be sure to adjust the length of the legs accordingly.

FIG 1

1 Take the five prepared boards for the worktop (630 mm long, 140 mm wide), and place them side by side so that the end grain in neighbouring planks runs in different directions.

Mark in the position of the biscuit joints at the centre and 50 mm from the ends. Set the biscuit jointer to 15 mm and cut the slots on the five boards. Blow out the dust and spread glue on the mating faces of the biscuits and the boards, and clamp up. Use three sash clamps, plus the G-clamps, to hold the joints in place (see Fig 1).

When the glue is completely dry, remove the clamps and move the slab to a clean, level surface. Finally, use the jigsaw, block plane and scraper plane to work the slab to a smooth, clean-edged finish, 630 mm square. Remove all traces of glue.

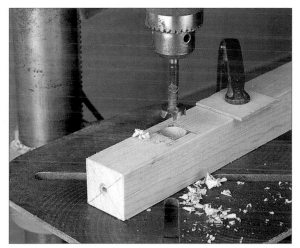

FIG 2

2 Take the four 710 mm legs and mark the top and bottom. Set out mortises 25 mm square, at centres 225 mm down from the top and 95 mm up from the bottom. Draw crossed diagonals to establish the position of the wheel bolts. Drill the mortises with the 25 mm forstner bit, to a depth of 40 mm. Drill holes in the ends of the legs to fit your wheel bolts (see Fig 2).

FIG 4

4 Take the four 550 mm stretchers and set out the tenons by measuring 40 mm from the ends. Set the mitre saw depth gauge to 2.5 mm and saw the tenon shoulders (see Fig 4). Use the chisel to pare the tenons to fit. Aim for a tight push-fit, with the shoulders of the tenon sitting square and flush with the face of the leg. Test it is square with the square.

FIG 3

3 Clamp the legs to the bench and use the bevel-edge chisel and the mallet to work the bored holes into crisp, blind mortises 25 mm square and 40 mm deep (see Fig 3). Scrape the bottom of the mortise to a clean finish and remove all the debris. Be careful not to lever the tool against the side of the mortise.

FIG 5

5 Mark out open rail mortises on the legs, at 75 mm long, 12 mm wide and 20 mm deep, and centred so that the rails are set 10 mm back from the face. Attach the router to its table, fit the 12 mm groove cutter, set the fence to 14 mm, clamp a depth-stop block made from an offcut at 75 mm, and rout the mortises (see Fig 5).

FIG 6

6 Mark the ends of the rails at 20 mm. Rout the stepped tenons, making them 20 mm long, 75 mm wide and 12 mm thick. Use the knife to whittle the stepped underside so that it fits into the 12 mm open mortise (see Fig 6).

FIG 7

7 Plane the worktop to a square finish with the smoothing plane. Use the biscuit jointer to cut grooves on the inside face of both side rails. Use the tenon saw to cut turnbuckles and screw blocks (see Fig 7) from scrap wood to fit.

Clear the workbench of accumulated clutter and use a vacuum cleaner to remove all small pieces of debris. If the top of your workbench is badly scarred or covered in hard blobs of glue, cover it with a sheet of clean plywood to work on. It is vital that the surface is perfectly clean. Set the worktop face down on the workbench or ply-

wood, and have a trial dry-run fitting of the legs, stretchers and rails (see Fig 7).

When you are happy with the way it all comes together, spread glue in the joints and clamp up. When the glue is dry, remove the clamps, screw the blocks and the turnbuckles in place to hold the worktop to the rails, and use the chisel and the sandpaper to remove all traces of dried glue.

TIP

To avoid drill chatter and friction burns when countersinking the holes, fix the drill's depth gauge to 5 mm and then swiftly and firmly run the countersink bit in and out. Make sure the drill is running at full speed before the bit strikes the wood.

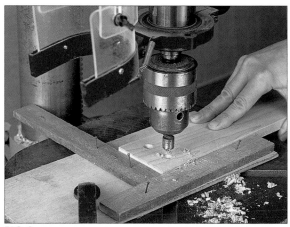

FIG 8

8 Take two of the shelf slats and mark out the position of the screwholes 25 mm from the ends – one with a single hole at the centre and the other with two holes 20 mm in from the sides. Double-check your measurements.

Use the two slats to build a jig from scrap wood, and then drill all the slats with the 5 mm twist bit and the pilot-countersink bit (see Fig 8).

Make sure, after every drilling, that you stop and use a brush to remove the sawdust from the corners of the jig. Work carefully so that the drill bit enters and exits leaving clean holes.

FIG 9

FIG 10

9 Clear all the dust and fragments of wood off the workbench and set the trolley upside-down on the bench, so that the ends of the legs are at a comfortable height. With the socket and wrench, bolt the wheels in place (see Fig 9). Go over the trolley with the block plane, cleaning up ends and skimming off sharp corners. Make sure that all traces of glue have been removed. To this end, take the trolley outside the workshop, so that you can view it in full daylight, and inspect all the areas around the joints. A good test is to brush the surface with white spirit, which will highlight any areas of glue. Finally, sweep up the debris and wipe the dust off with a cotton cloth.

10 Move to a clean area and brush the whole trolley with a thin coat of Danish oil, working over the frame with the worktop in place and the ten loose slats.

Set the two-hole slats to bridge the stretchers, so that they are hard up against the legs with the ends flush (see Fig 10). Drill 3 mm pilot holes and fix the slats in place with the stainless-steel screws. Set out the single-hole slats with a spacing of 30 mm and repeat the screwing procedure. To ensure that the spacing is uniform, cut a strip of waste 30 mm wide, and set it between neighbouring slats before driving the screws home. Screw the stainless-steel rail in place.

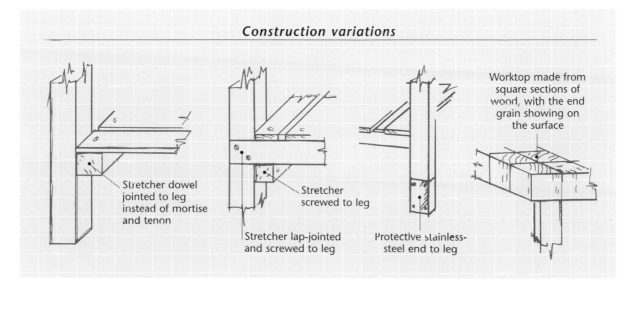

Construction variations

Stretcher dowel jointed to leg instead of mortise and tenon

Stretcher screwed to leg

Stretcher lap-jointed and screwed to leg

Protective stainless-steel end to leg

Worktop made from square sections of wood, with the end grain showing on the surface

French cupboard

This pretty little herb cupboard was inspired by a cupboard that we saw about twenty years ago when on a walking holiday in southern France. We looked though a farmhouse window and there it was, perfectly captured in a shaft of sunlight. It was a very simple construction, really not much more than a fruit crate – perhaps it was even made from scrap wood.

Our design is lifted above the ordinary by beautifully delicate curves at top and bottom, a colourwashed finish, and a whittled handle that doubles as a catch. The cupboard is made from good-quality pine tongue-and-groove boards for the front, back, sides and shelves; pine sections for the door battens and shelf supports inside, to hold the whole thing together; and an offcut for the handle. The surface is colourwashed with a mixture of acrylic paint and water, and finally wiped over with teak oil. We chose a mix of blue and green to achieve a greenish tinge, but you can opt for any colour that appeals, such as a strong red, or even a limewashed finish.

— Essential Tools —

workbench with vice, pencil, rule, square, smoothing plane, screwdriver, scroll saw, sanding block, mitre saw, 7 mm counter-bore bit with a plug cutter to match, knife, electric drill, 10 mm and 3 mm twist bits, awl, 2 paintbrushes

OTHER USEFUL TOOLS
cordless screwdriver, power sander, marking knife

French cupboard

200 mm

338 mm

140 mm

650 mm

100 mm

700 mm

100 mm

100 mm

80 mm   89 mm   89 mm   80 mm

You'll need to know

SCREWING
p.24

CUTTING CURVED SHAPES
p.18

WHITTLING
p.25

Materials

pine (see cutting list)

50+ countersunk steel screws:
35 mm x no. 8

sandpaper grades 80 and 150

2 surface-mounted brass hinges
(design and size to suit) with screws to fit

acrylic paint: colour to suit

teak oil

Cutting List

all pieces cut from pine

4 pieces of tongue-and-groove
700 x 89 x 15 mm (front boards, consisting
of 2 doors and 2 side pieces)

4 pieces of tongue-and-groove
650 x 89 x 15 mm (back boards)

4 pieces of tongue-and-groove
650 x 89 x 15 mm (side boards)

3 pieces 312 x 170 x 18 mm (shelves)

8 pieces 160 x 30 x 18 mm
(2 door battens and 6 shelf supports)

If you want to carve a more complex catch than this one (which is made of leftover scraps), consider using a piece of easy-to-carve lime.

FIG 1

FIG 2

1 Study the design and note how all the boards that meet at the corners have been reduced in width. Now take the smoothing plane and trim the boards to size (see Fig 1).

2 Take the two boards that make the door and screw them together with two 160 mm door battens. Use two staggered screws on each board width (see Fig 2).

FIG 3

3 Set the four front boards together (the two doors at centre and a side piece on either side), spring the rule across the top and draw out the curved profile (see Fig 2). Get help if needed. Repeat this procedure for the other end.

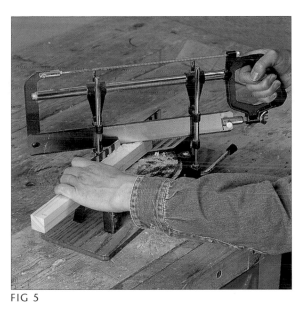

FIG 5

5 Take the six 160 mm shelf supports (two to support each shelf, two to support the top of the cupboard and two to support the bottom) and use the mitre saw to cut one end of each piece to 45° (see Fig 5).

FIG 4

4 Take the door (all screwed together) and with the curved ends clearly marked out, very carefully cut the curved profile on the scroll saw (see Fig 4). Cut the two side boards in the same way. Sand the sawn edges to a smooth, slightly rounded and blurred finish.

FIG 6

6 Take the three 312 mm shelf boards and screw the 160 mm shelf supports to the ends, so that the square end of the support is flush with the back edge of the shelf board (see Fig 6). Use the block and sandpaper to rub all edges and ends to a smooth finish.

FIG 7

7 Screw the three shelf boards to the paired side boards (see Fig 7). Note that the middle shelf is placed so that the supports are on the underside, with the mitred ends looking to what will be the front of the cupboard. Screw the other two side boards in place.

FIG 8

8 Screw the four back boards in place, with screws running through into the edges of the shelves and the side boards (see Fig 8). The screws should be flush with the surface. Screw the front of the cupboard in place, this time sinking the holes with the counter-bore bit so that the screws will lie well below the surface.

FIG 9

9 Whittle the three components that make the door catch – the piece that screws to the side of the cupboard, the latch and the central swivel. There is no need to copy our design exactly, just study it to see how it functions and then go for a similar form. Drill through the latch with the 10 mm bit and slide the central swivel in place. Drill a 3 mm hole through the side of the unit and fix with a dowel whittled from an offcut (make it 100 mm long and 3 mm in diameter). Continue carving the catch components until the form becomes a pleasing whole (see Fig 9). Use a fold of sandpaper wrapped around a stick to sculpt the wood to a smooth shape and finish.

FIG 10

10 Set the door in place, spike the screw-holes with the awl and screw the hinges in place. Depending upon the size of your chosen hinges, position one about 140 mm down from the top and the other about 100 mm up from the bottom (see Fig 10). Use a fold of fine-grade sandpaper to blur the surface of the brass hinges and dull the shine.

FIG 11

11 Screw the catch to the side of the cupboard and use it to establish the position of the swivel latch. Mark the pivot point with a pencil, and drill with the 10 mm bit. Slide the central peg in place (see Fig 11). Drill a hole in the peg with the 3 mm bit, on the inside face of the door. Whittle a pin with the knife and slide it through to hold the latch in place.

Rub down all the surfaces with the graded sandpapers. Dilute the paint in water and colour-wash the cupboard. When it is dry, sand all the surfaces to a smooth finish – cutting through the paint to reveal the grain – and wipe all the surfaces with teak oil. With the plug cutter, cut little plugs from scrap wood and glue them in the counter-bored holes to cover the screwheads.

TIP

It's a good idea to experiment with colourwashing before you tackle the cupboard. Thin some acrylic paint with water and paint a piece of scrap wood, then sand and oil as described. If you want the colour to be lighter or darker, you simply add more water or paint accordingly. Remember that sawn edges and light grain absorb more colour and look darker.

Construction variations

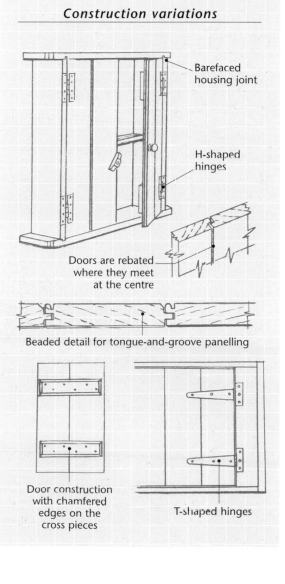

Barefaced housing joint

H-shaped hinges

Doors are rebated where they meet at the centre

Beaded detail for tongue-and-groove panelling

Door construction with chamfered edges on the cross pieces

T-shaped hinges

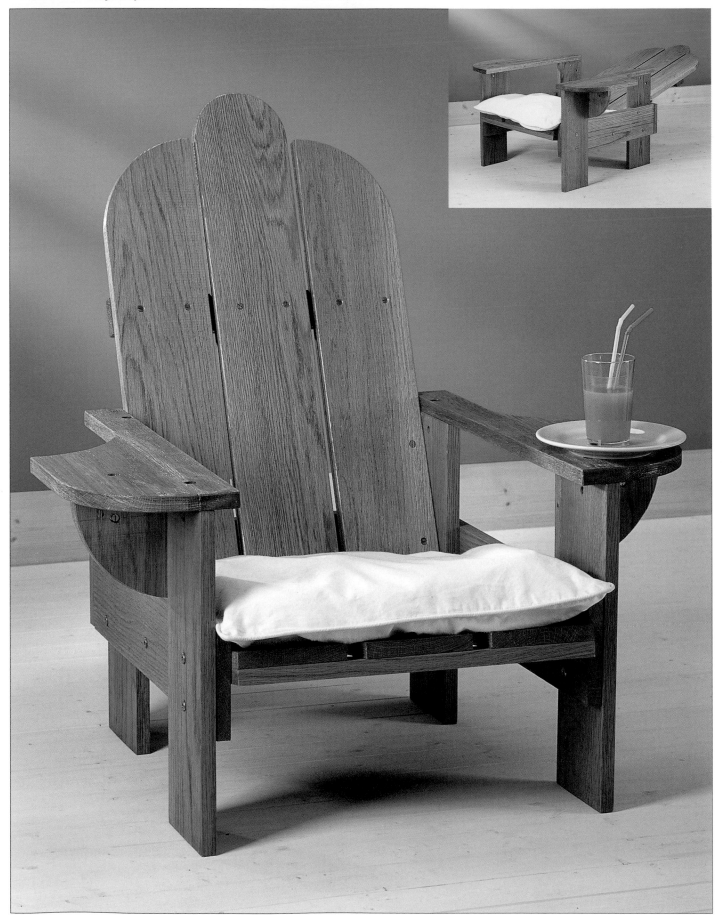

Adjustable porch chair

If you would like to build a swift and easy porch chair, this classic "crate" design is sure to please. The project draws its inspiration from the work of Gerrit Rietveld (1888–1957), the Dutch designer and architect, and member of the De Stijl group, who developed designs that could be made from salvaged wood. It's a stylish chair, perfect for the porch, conservatory or studio. The back can be adjusted. If you want to relax and stretch out for a doze, you simply withdraw the two gate bolts in order to lower the back.

The chair is made from American oak, and the boards are jointed with screws and toggle fasteners. The great thing about the design is that the whole chair can be made without having to cut any joints. The boards are simply butted or sandwiched and then fitted with toggle fasteners running through the thickness. The two H-frames that make up the arms are linked by the seat frame in such a way that the back can be fixed in either an upright or horizontal mode. To finish the surface of the wood, it is vigorously wire-brushed to give it a weathered texture and wiped with Danish oil.

Essential Tools

workbench with vice, compasses, pencil, rule, square, G-clamps, bench drill press, 10 mm and 15 mm forstner bits, 5 mm twist bit, scroll saw, 2 sash clamps, block plane, sanding block, wire brush, paintbrush, pilot-countersink bit, screwdriver, hacksaw, metal file, allen key to fit the hex-heads

OTHER USEFUL TOOLS
cordless screwdriver, power sander, electric drill, dividers, marking knife

Adjustable porch chair

**You'll need
to know**

DRILLING HOLES
p.19

CUTTING CURVED
SHAPES
p.18

SPECIAL FINISHES
p.27

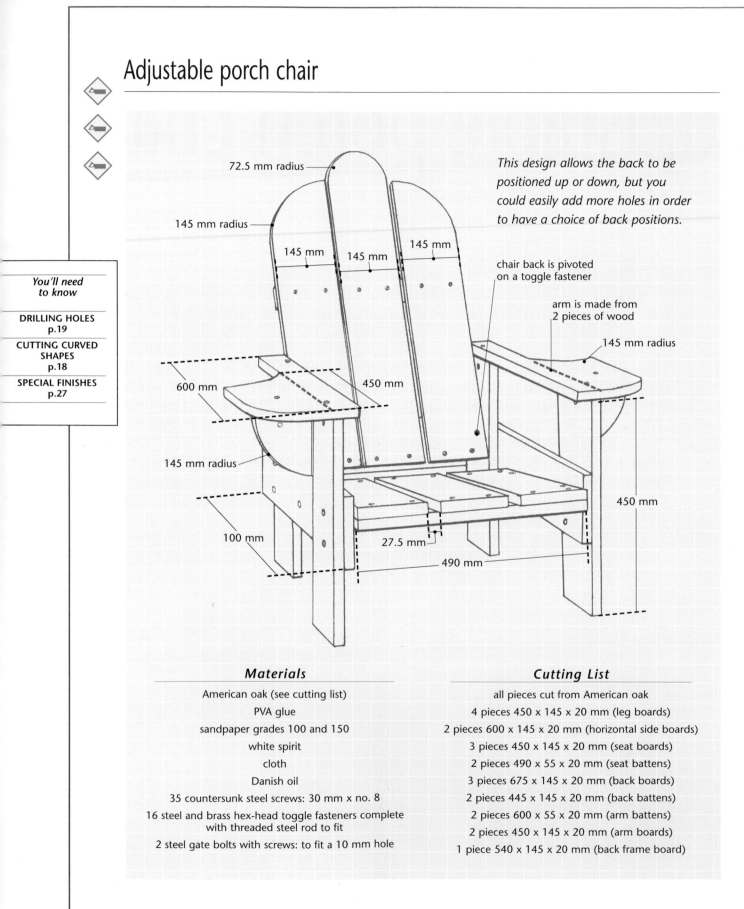

72.5 mm radius

145 mm radius

145 mm

145 mm

145 mm

This design allows the back to be positioned up or down, but you could easily add more holes in order to have a choice of back positions.

chair back is pivoted on a toggle fastener

arm is made from 2 pieces of wood

145 mm radius

600 mm

450 mm

145 mm radius

450 mm

100 mm

27.5 mm

490 mm

Materials

American oak (see cutting list)

PVA glue

sandpaper grades 100 and 150

white spirit

cloth

Danish oil

35 countersunk steel screws: 30 mm x no. 8

16 steel and brass hex-head toggle fasteners complete with threaded steel rod to fit

2 steel gate bolts with screws: to fit a 10 mm hole

Cutting List

all pieces cut from American oak

4 pieces 450 x 145 x 20 mm (leg boards)

2 pieces 600 x 145 x 20 mm (horizontal side boards)

3 pieces 450 x 145 x 20 mm (seat boards)

2 pieces 490 x 55 x 20 mm (seat battens)

3 pieces 675 x 145 x 20 mm (back boards)

2 pieces 445 x 145 x 20 mm (back battens)

2 pieces 600 x 55 x 20 mm (arm battens)

2 pieces 450 x 145 x 20 mm (arm boards)

1 piece 540 x 145 x 20 mm (back frame board)

FIG 1

1 Study the working drawing and work out the position of the various drilled holes. Build a simple jig using workshop offcuts, and clamp the jig to the bench drill press with G-clamps. Set to work drilling the blind holes to fit the brass hex-heads, using the 15 mm forstner bit (see Fig 1). Drill to a depth of 5 mm.

FIG 3

3 Take the three 675 mm back boards, decide on the best ends and faces, and use the compasses to set out the top details. Use a radius of 72.5 mm for the middle board, and 145 mm for the other two (see Fig 3). If you can get hold of an adjustable compass to use, it is better because the legs stay put and will not slip.

FIG 2

2 Change to the 10 mm forstner bit and continue the hole through the thickness of the wood (see Fig 2). Re-run this procedure for all the hex-head holes. Use the 10 mm forstner bit for the toggle holes, and the 5 mm twist bit for the screw and rod holes.

FIG 4

4 Fit a new fine-toothed blade in the scroll saw, make adjustments to ensure maximum tension, and then fret out the top ends of the three back boards (see Fig 4). If you work at a slow pace, the sawn edge will turn out to be so smooth that it will hardly need sanding.

FIG 5

5 Take one of the 450 mm arm boards, set the compasses to a radius of 145 mm and scribe the back end of the board with the quarter-circle curve that makes the design. Fret out the curve on the scroll saw and keep the piece of quarter-circle waste for the arm bracket. Take the fretted arm board and one of the 600 mm arm battens, smear glue on mating side faces and clamp them together with the sash clamps (see Fig 5). Be careful not to over-tighten the clamps so that they buckle. When the glue is dry, scribe an identical quarter-circle curve on the front end of the arm and fret it out on the scroll saw. Re-run this procedure for the other arm.

FIG 6

6 Use the block plane and sandpaper to work the end-grain surfaces of all components to a good finish, chamfering all the corners and edges. Wire-brush all surfaces. Remove the dust with a cloth dampened in white spirit and brush all the surfaces with Danish oil (see Fig 6).

FIG 7

7 To build the seat, set the two 490 mm seat battens flat on the bench and bridge them with the three 450 mm seat boards. Use a piece of wood 27.5 mm thick to space the boards precisely the same distance apart. Make checks with the square and rule, drill screwholes with the pilot-countersink bit and fix the boards in place with screws (see Fig 7).

TIP

Depending upon the manufacturer, hex-head toggle fastners come in many shapes, types and sizes. They may be made of stainless steel or plastic rather than brass, and the hex-head size may differ. So you might well need to use a different-sized drill bit to suit the particular design and size of your fitting. Buy the fittings and experiment on scrap wood to ascertain the necessary drill size.

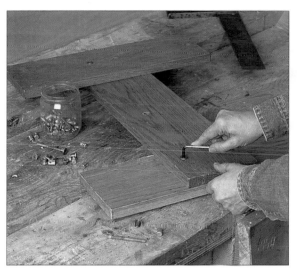

FIG 8

FIG 9

9 Screw the arm bracket to the inside edge of the front leg board and fit the arm board with the toggle fasteners (see Fig 9). Repeat on the other arm. Check with the square.

8 To build the side H-frames, take two 450 mm vertical leg boards and bridge them with the 600 mm horizontal side board (with one leg under and the other over). Slide the toggle fasteners in place (hex-heads, toggle and threaded rod cut to length with the hacksaw and tidied up with the file), and use the allen key to tighten up just enough to grip. Make checks with the square, and complete necessary adjustments to the alignment. Clench the toggle fasteners to make the whole thing stable (see Fig 8). Re-run this procedure for the other H-frame. While the two H-frames are identical in every respect, they are also mirror image copies of each other, as are the arms of most chairs.

FIG 10

10 Finally, when you have pivoted the seat back on the toggle fasteners – as shown in the working drawing – and screwed the horizontal back board in place, fix the two gate bolts (see Fig 10).

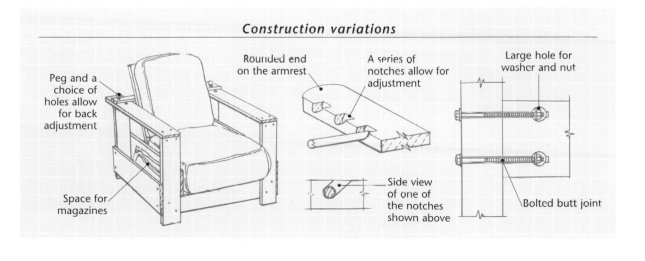

Construction variations

Peg and a choice of holes allow for back adjustment

Rounded end on the armrest

A series of notches allow for adjustment

Large hole for washer and nut

Space for magazines

Side view of one of the notches shown above

Bolted butt joint

Log trough

This design is a coming together of many troughs that we have seen over the years. It looks a little like a dough trough once spotted in a baker's shop in Leicestershire, the handle owes its shape to a New England knife tray in the American Museum in Bath, but most of all, this trough draws its inspiration from an early nineteenth-century washing trough that we found in our house in Cornwall. All these troughs have certain things in common: a characteristic canted boat-like shape, the way the pierced handle strip is fixed to the end board, and the colour green. The appealing thing about them is the fact that while the woodworker needed to do no more than make a functional box – for washing clothes, baking and suchlike – he found time to make it into a decorative form.

This log trough is made from pine and plywood. The fretted handle strip is screwed to the end board, while the sides are nailed to the ends. It's a surprisingly challenging project. If you are interested in building other troughs and need inspiration, visit a rural life museum to see the beautiful troughs used in the house, dairy and garden.

Essential Tools

workbench with vice and holdfast, compasses, pencils, rule, square, bevel gauge, bench drill press, 5 mm and 8 mm twist bits, scroll saw, 2 short sash clamps, screwdriver, spokeshave, block plane, router and router table, 10 mm groove cutter, sanding block, medium pin hammer, paintbrush

OTHER USEFUL TOOLS
cordless screwdriver, power sander, electric drill, dividers, marking knife

Log trough

You'll need to know

CUTTING CURVED SHAPES p.18

ROUTING A GROOVE p.22

NAILING AND PINNING p.24

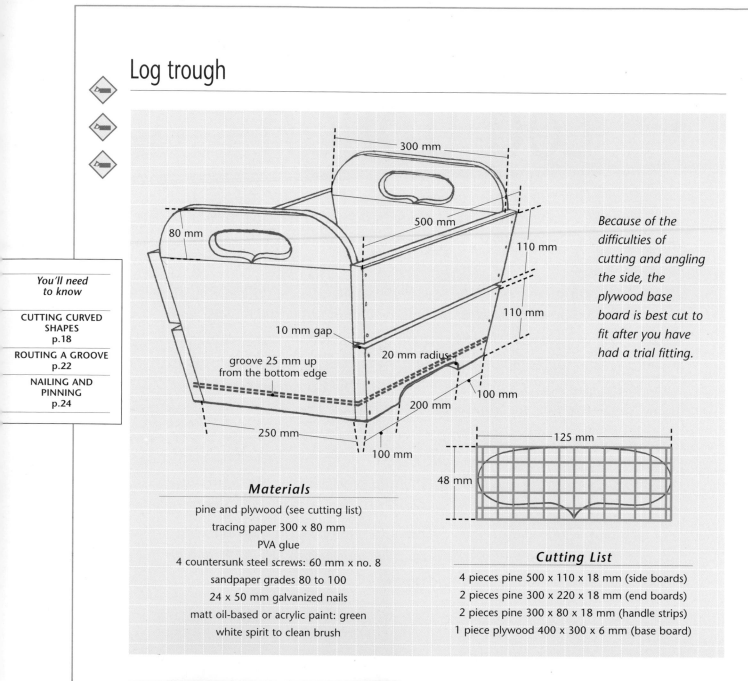

300 mm

500 mm

80 mm

110 mm

110 mm

10 mm gap

groove 25 mm up from the bottom edge

20 mm radius

200 mm

100 mm

250 mm

100 mm

125 mm

48 mm

Because of the difficulties of cutting and angling the side, the plywood base board is best cut to fit after you have had a trial fitting.

Materials

pine and plywood (see cutting list)
tracing paper 300 x 80 mm
PVA glue
4 countersunk steel screws: 60 mm x no. 8
sandpaper grades 80 to 100
24 x 50 mm galvanized nails
matt oil-based or acrylic paint: green
white spirit to clean brush

Cutting List

4 pieces pine 500 x 110 x 18 mm (side boards)
2 pieces pine 300 x 220 x 18 mm (end boards)
2 pieces pine 300 x 80 x 18 mm (handle strips)
1 piece plywood 400 x 300 x 6 mm (base board)

FIG 1

1 Take your piece of tracing paper – the same size as the handle strip – and fold it in half along its length so that the crease becomes the centre-line. Use a soft pencil to carefully draw one half of the shape of the handle on the tracing paper. Establish the centre-lines on the two handle strips. With a hard pencil, press-transfer the shape of the handle through to both pieces of wood. Shade in the waste so that there is no doubting what needs to be cut away (see Fig 1). You might need to adjust the handle to fit your hand.

FIG 2

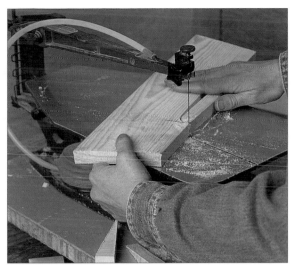

FIG 4

2 Take the four side boards and use the bevel gauge, rule and square to draw the overall shape of the angled side. Use the rule and compasses to draw the foot detail on the two bottom side boards (see Fig 2).

4 Cut out the shape of the side boards on the scroll saw (see Fig 4). Work at a steady pace, cutting to the waste side of the drawn line. Next, cut out the shape of the two end boards. Pencil-label all the component parts.

FIG 3

FIG 5

3 Take the handle strips and drill the screw-holes. Drill the 5 mm pilot holes completely through the wood, then re-drill the hole with an 8 mm bit to a depth of 30 mm (so the screw can be sunk). Cut out the shape of the handle on the scroll saw. When you come to cut the handle hole, enter and exit the blade where the pointed detail meets the edge (see Fig 3).

5 Take one end board and a fretted handle strip, smear glue on mating edges and clamp up. Drive the screws down the pilot holes and then remove the two clamps (see Fig 5). Repeat this procedure for the other end.

FIG 6

FIG 8

7 Use the block plane, set to a fine cut, to swiftly chamfer all sides and ends of the side boards (see Fig 7). Don't aim for a really exquisite finish – small irregularities are in keeping with the style of the project.

6 When the glue is dry, set the end board in the vice. Use the spokeshave to plane the top edge of the end board to a slightly rounded, smooth finish (see Fig 6). Work from centre to side so you do not split the wood by running the blade into the end grain.

Take a fold of sandpaper and rub the inside edges of the handle hole to a good, smooth finish. Concentrate your efforts on the top of the hole, so the handle is easy and comfortable to hold.

8 Attach the router to its table, fit the 10 mm groove cutter and set the fence to 25 mm. Run the two end boards and the side boards through to cut a groove 10 mm wide and 6 mm deep, 25 mm up from the bottom edge (see Fig 8). Use a push-stick to feed the wood through and keep your fingers out of harm's way.

FIG 7

FIG 9

9 Have a dry run put-together in order to decide (by eye) how much the edges of the two end boards need to be angled back. Then pair the two boards back to back in the vice, and use the block plane to angle back from the mating faces (see Fig 9).

TIP

While in many ways this is an easy project to make, the final fitting of the base and sides is a bit of a challenge. In the first instance, it may help to put the whole trough together with short pins, perhaps with a friend's help, and then to adjust the various edges for best fit. Angle the nails slightly so that they can't be pulled out easily.

FIG 10

10 Trim the plywood base board to fit your trough. Give all the component parts a swift rub-down with sandpaper, then start nailing the whole thing together (see Fig 10). As the nailing progresses, you will see that the side and end boards cant (lean) out to the extent that the 6 mm-thick plywood base becomes a tight fit in the 10 mm-wide grooves.

You might even need to ease the base by chamfering the edges of the routed grooves slightly. When the whole box is nailed together, give it a coat of paint on all surfaces.

When the paint is completely dry, sand selected faces and edges to cut through the paint. Concentrate your efforts on areas that would, in the normal course of events, receive most wear.

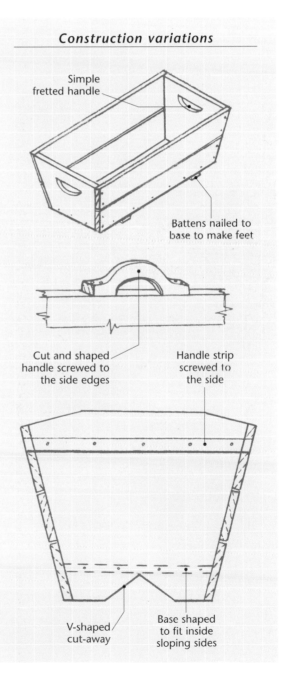

Construction variations

Simple fretted handle

Battens nailed to base to make feet

Cut and shaped handle screwed to the side edges

Handle strip screwed to the side

V-shaped cut-away

Base shaped to fit inside sloping sides

SUPPLIERS

United Kingdom

Tool manufacturers
Black & Decker
210 Bath Road
Slough
Berkshire
SL1 3YD
Tel: 01753 511 234

Stanley UK Ltd
The Stanley Works
Woodside
Sheffield
Yorkshire
S3 9PD
Tel: 0114 276 8888

Tool retailers
Tilgear
Bridge House
69 Station Road
Cuffley, Potters Bar
Hertfordshire
EN6 4TG
Tel: 01707 873 434

S J Carter Tools Ltd
Gloucester House
10 Camberwell New Road
London
SE5 0TA
Tel: 020 7587 1222

Router tables and accessories
Trend Machinery
& Cutting Tools Ltd
Unit 6
Odhams Trading Estate
St. Albans Rd, Watford
Hertfordshire
WD24 7RY
Tel: 01923 249 911
Email: mailserver@trend.co.uk

Ironmongery
Isaac Lord
181 Desborough Road
High Wycombe
Buckinghamshire
HP11 2QN
Tel: 01494 462 121

Hardwood retailers and timberyards
South London Hardwoods
390 Sydenham Road
Croydon
Surrey
CR0 2EA
Tel: 020 8683 0292

North Heigham Sawmills Ltd
26 Paddock Street
Norwich
Norfolk
NR2 4TW
Tel: 01603 622 978

General DIY stores
(outlets nationwide):
B & Q Plc
Head Office:
Portswood House
1 Hampshire Corporate Park
Chandlers Ford
Eastleigh
Hampshire
SO53 3YX
Tel: 0845 609 6688

Focus Wickes Ltd
Head Office:
Gawsworth House
Westmere Drive
Crewe
Cheshire
CW1 6XB
Tel: 01270 501 555

Homebase Ltd
Beddington House
Railway Approach
Wallington
Surrey
SM6 0HB
Tel: 020 8784 7200

For further listings of retailers, the best place to get a national overview is from the many **woodworking magazines:**

Furniture & Cabinet Making
Guild of Master Craftsmen
166 High Street
Lewes
Sussex
BN7 1XU
Tel: 01273 477 374

Traditional Woodworking
The Well House
High Street
Burton-on-Trent
Staffordshire
DE14 1JQ
Tel: 01283 742 970

Practical Woodworking
and *The Woodworker*
Nexus House
Azalea Drive
Swanley
Kent
BR8 8HU
Tel: 01858 435 344

South Africa

Timber suppliers
Federated Timbers
14 McKenzie Street
Industrial Sites
Bloemfontein 9301
Tel: 051 447 3171
Fax: 051 447 5053
(Outlets nationwide)

P G Bison
4–5 Kwaford Road
Port Elizabeth 6001
Tel: 041 453 1250
Fax: 041 543 5046
(Outlets nationwide)

DIY and hardware
Hardware Centre
14 Brëe Street
Cape Town 8001
Tel: 021 421 7358
Fax: 021 419 6792

Hardware Centre
Union Main Centre
Old Main Road
Pinetown
Durban 3610
Tel: 031 702 2629
Fax: 031 702 2581

Wardkiss Paint
& Hardware Centre
329 Sydney Road
Durban 4001
Tel: 031 205 1551
Fax: 031 205 2554
(Outlets nationwide)

Tool retailers
J & J Sales
38 Argyle Street
East London 5201
Tel: 043 743 3380
Fax: 043 743 5432

Tooltrick
55A Bok Street
Pietersburg 0699
Tel: 015 295 5982
Fax: 015 295 6151

Australia

DIY stores
Mitre 10
319 George Street
Sydney 2000
Tel: 02 9262 1435
Customer service:
1800 803 304
(Outlets nationwide)

BBC Hardware
Head Office, Bldg. A
Cnr. Cambridge
and Chester Streets
Epping
NSW 2121
Tel: 02 9876 0888
(Outlets nationwide)

Timber suppliers
ABC Timbers and
Building Supplies Pty Ltd
46 Auburn Road
Regents Park 2143
Tel: 02 9645 2511

Australian Treated
Timber Sales
Brisbane 4000
Tel: 01 800 06 0685

Bowens Timber
and Building Supplies
135–173 Macaulay Road
North Melbourne 3051
Tel: 03 9328 1041

New Zealand

DIY stores
Mitre 10
Head Office:
182 Wairau Road
Glenfield
Auckland
Tel: 09 443 9900
(Branches nationwide)

Placemakers Support Office
150 Marua Road
Private Bag 14942
Panmure
Auckland
Tel: 09 525 5100

Handles, hinges and castors
Hammer Hardware stores
are located nationwide. Look
in your telephone book for
your nearest branch or consult
www.whitepages.co.nz

Rosenfeld Kidson
513 Mt. Wellington Highway
Mt. Wellington
Auckland
Tel: 09 573 0503
Fax 09 573 0504
(Timber merchants)

CONVERSION CHART

To convert the metric measurements given in this book to imperial measurements, simply multiply the figure given in the text by the relevant number shown in the table alongside. Bear in mind that conversions will not necessarily work out exactly, and you will need to round the figure up or down slightly. (Do not use a combination of metric and imperial measurements – for accuracy, keep to one system.)

To convert	Multiply by
millimetres to inches	0.0394
metres to feet	3.28
metres to yards	1.093
sq millimetres to sq inches	0.00155
sq metres to sq feet	10.76
sq metres to sq yards	1.195
cu metres to cu feet	35.31
cu metres to cu yards	1.308
grams to pounds	0.0022
kilograms to pounds	2.2046
litres to gallons	0.26

INDEX

page numbers for photographs and illustrations are shown in italics